OUR BRAVE NEW WORLD

*Hoover Institution gratefully acknowledges
the following foundations for their
significant support of the*

National Security Forum

LYNDE AND HARRY BRADLEY FOUNDATION

ROBERT R. MCCORMICK TRIBUNE FOUNDATION, CHICAGO

*Hoover Institution
gratefully acknowledges the*

ROBERT R. MCCORMICK
TRIBUNE FOUNDATION, CHICAGO

for its generous support of this book project.

EDITED BY WLADYSLAW PLESZCZYNSKI

Our Brave
New World

Essays on
the Impact of
September 11

HOOVER INSTITUTION PRESS

Stanford University   Stanford, California

www.hoover.org

Hoover Institution Press Publication No. 514

First printing 2002
08   07   06   05   04   03   02   9   8   7   6   5   4   3   2   1

Manufactured in the United States of America
The paper used in this publication meets the minimum requirements
of American National Standard for Information Sciences—Permanence
of Paper for Printed Library Materials, ANSI Z39.48-1984. ♾

Library of Congress Cataloging-in-Publication Data
Our brave new world : essays on the impact of September 11 /
edited by Wladyslaw Pleszczynski.
    p.   cm. (Hoover Institution Press publication ; no. 514)
Includes bibliographical references and index.
ISBN 0-8179-3902-4 (paperback) — ISBN 0-8179-3901-6 (casebound)
    1. Civilization, Modern—21st century.   2. World politics—21st
century.   3. September 11 Terrorist Attacks, 2001.   I. Pleszczynski,
Wladyslaw, 1949–   .   II. Hoover Institution Press publication ; 514.
CB430 .O928   2002
973.931—dc21   2002068566

CONTENTS

Introduction   vii
    Wladyslaw Pleszczynski

The New New World Order:
America and the New Geopolitics   1
    Anne Applebaum

The World That Didn't Change—Much:
Partisanship and the Politics of National Security After 9/11   21
    Byron York

A New Round of Anger and Humiliation: Islam After 9/11   41
    Daniel Pipes

What We Are Fighting For: The Example of Pericles   63
    Roger Kimball

Keen About Death: The Lost Language of National Honor   83
    James Bowman

Hollywood Searches for a New Script:
Popular Culture After September 11   105
    John Podhoretz

New York, New York: America's Hero   119
    John Corry

Contributors   137

Index   139

WLADYSLAW PLESZCZYNSKI

Introduction

IT WAS A NIGHTMARE right before our eyes. Each of us remembers exactly how it unfolded and where we were and what we were doing and how we reacted when the realization set in that we had been attacked in the vilest and cruelest way.

That morning I was working in my home in a quiet northern Virginia suburb. At some point after nine o'clock I heard a distant thud. I assumed that someone was having a big tree cut down. A heavy felled bough often sounds like that when it hits the turf. But several minutes later my older son called from his high school a few miles away. He was making sure I hadn't gone into Washington that morning. Then he told me to turn on the television.

When I did, the screen communicated an unimaginable, unforgettable image: a World Trade Center tower standing alone and on fire. First thought: Why is there only one tower? Second thought: Could it be . . .—but the thought is interrupted when the screen does in fact show two towers. Then out of nowhere a jetliner slices into one of them. It's hard to make sense of what the announcers are saying. Then that second tower collapses, and again the screen is showing a single burning tower. In time I would understand that television was already running replays of the attack on and collapse of the second tower while the first tower still stood.

If piecing together what had occurred and was occurring caused momentary confusions on September 11, there was immediate clarity in most everyone's response to the attacks on New York and Washington. Evacuation, search, and rescue from the outset saved countless lives even as it cost New York's selfless firemen unfathomable losses in a day of unthinkable losses. The heroism on display on September 11 rivals any in our history. In this volume lifelong New Yorker John Corry records a city at its most incredible.

But something else occurred right away, in a larger sense. The moment most Americans absorbed what was happening, their reactions did not dwell on denial or disbelief or other forms of evasive unacceptance. To the contrary, all such instincts were quickly suppressed if indulged in at all. A different reaction kicked in: We see what has happened. What are the facts? What are our options? What do we do now? What's next? Who is behind the attacks? When do we strike back? How do we prevent any further attacks? Variations on these questions were endless, but they all bespoke a national determination to respond to the unprecedented shock with cool purpose and steely resolve. As Daniel Pipes so eloquently captures the phenomenon, an aroused democracy is a sight to see.

Concomitant was an even larger instantaneous understanding about September 11. It was a historic turning point. Common sense told us so. One day we are blissfully safe and unsuspecting. The next we have been violated as never before in

memory. Life cannot be the same again. It has instilled a new
seriousness. Yes, the passage of time would ease the shock, the
grief, the pain, and the anger. The strong U.S. response to the
attacks also helped restore a sense of security, and likely created
many deterrents against future attacks. But trauma leaves its
mark. The possibility of further attacks remains an open concern. Whatever form they might take would surprise no one. A
vigilant nation has no illusions. It carries on, as it must, stronger
if sadder but with renewed purpose and lasting memory—and
a permanent sense of loss.

In the American Enterprise Institute's 2002 Francis Boyer
Lecture delivered in February, Norman Podhoretz opened by
questioning "whether 9/11 hurled us into a new era of American
history. Certainly this is how it seemed . . ." Whether it will
continue to seem so is now open to some dispute. Yet in that
very same lecture Mr. Podhoretz cited a passage from a 1947
essay by George F. Kennan in which Kennan expressed "a
certain gratitude for a Providence which, by providing the
American people with this implacable challenge, has made
their entire security as a nation dependent on their pulling
themselves together and accepting the responsibilities of moral
and political leadership that history plainly intended them to
bear."

Americans pulled together to wage the Cold War, and since
September they have pulled together to support the war on
terrorism. How long we remain pulled together we cannot
know. As Roger Kimball notes, even "the foreseeable future"
is not something we take for granted anymore. All we know for
certain is that Americans retain an ability to unite when they
most need to. They will defend their security—and once they
sense they are secure again will feel free to go off in different
directions. That's what a free people do.

The essays in this collection were commissioned in the first

months after September 11, when the post-attack intensity was
at its freshest and most raw. They were written and completed
months later, when a certain balance had returned to American
life—in no small part because of the unity and purpose that
sustained us in those first post-attack months. But like any
unprecedented historic jolt, September 11 continues to roil our
collective mind. We continue to ponder what changed that
historic day. What remained of the old? What is truly new?
Initially it was tempting to think that we could quickly dispense
with the worst of the pre-attack world, whether the frivolous-
ness of our cultural pursuits or the fecklessness of our politics
and foreign policy. But then we learned that the past conditions
are present in permanent ways. Change can only take us so far.
We remain who we are, and what is thought to be lasting change
can always turn out to be no more than an accretion that doesn't
stick.

The clearest areas of discernible change have come in our
foreign and domestic policies. In her essay Anne Applebaum
captures our new geopolitics: their unmistakable new definition, the challenges, the dangers—and the sense that we have
only seen the opening stage of a long-term realignment. This
revolution in foreign policy will remain the overriding issue of
our public life, no matter how much our chronic reluctance to
engage the world will try to cloud that perception.

In our domestic politics, as Byron York reports, partisan
considerations have remained as strong as before, with the exception of national security matters where public expectations
temper partisanship well before it reaches the water's edge.
Parodoxically, the president's duty to lead on foreign policy
gives him a political advantage his congressional opponents
can't match. By the new year they were responding with an
ever sharper voice on domestic issues, and even probing for
openings on national security matters. Against a president en-

joying strong national support, one sensed they were doing so at their own political risk.

As Daniel Pipes demonstrates, the Islamic world has gone through a more turbulent patch since September 11. The disproportionate influence that the radical Islamist movement imposed on that world well before al-Qaeda's attacks on the United States was strengthened further by terrorism's stunning success of 9/11—but only until a revived America turned the tables to bring about 11/9 and the ouster of al-Qaeda's Taliban protectors in Afghanistan. As never before, it is understood that American assertiveness is the main deterrent against Islamist terror, and a stabilizing force in a cultural sphere long beset by too many historical demons.

If Islam remains tormented and disheveled by the many unfortunate turns in its history, of which the aftermath of September 11 is only the latest in a long series of humiliating disappointments, America has tended to evade greater confrontation not only with its own immediate history but with the history of the civilization to which it belongs and the history of mankind even more broadly understood. When we react it is more by instinct and intuition. Two essayists seize the opportunity September 11 has opened to reflect in the most profound sense on what it is we are fighting for, as Roger Kimball puts it, and why we are fighting, despite, as James Bowman explains, having lost our ability to speak the language of honor—or to understand an enemy motivated by the most primitive form of the same language.

There is instructive uplift in Mr. Kimball's historical reflections, whether on the humbling enormity of a single event or the fragility of a civilization that treasures freedom and tolerance. Mr. Bowman is less confident, if only because our opinion-shaping elites have drifted so far away from the common understandings and meanings that should unite us all. The danger remains that we will go on acting on instincts we cannot, or are not allowed to, put words to.

Then there is Hollywood, long the purveyor of a popular culture antithetical to any deep commitments to American institutions or even to the idea of America the Beautiful. September 11 left it stunned and not a little clueless. The result, as John Podhoretz reports in series of memorable vignettes, has been both silly and embarrassing. America's popular culture remains on hold, uncertain if it has anything but its old habits to fall back on, yet sensing that perhaps, just perhaps, they will no longer do.

What a contrast New York has offered, though the lessons it taught have not been fully appreciated. Much has been made of the sterling leadership Mayor Giuliani displayed after the attacks, which above all won him the adulation of the very same media and artistic elite that had hounded him throughout his tenure. As John Corry ever so gently reminds us, there was nothing different about Giuliani on September 11. His mayoralty had in fact left New York well prepared to withstand the worst. Not coincidentally, New York's neighborhoods of ordinary folk led the way as well. Once again we were reminded where America's real strengths lie.

The strengths of this book are its seven individual contributors, and I trust readers will be as grateful to them as I am for their astute and thoughtful essays. I would also like to thank John Raisian, director of the Hoover Institution, for encouraging me to undertake this project and for the inspiration and support he gave me every step of the way. Together, we wish to acknowledge the significant support of the Robert R. McCormick Tribune Foundation. Its partnership made this project possible.

ANNE APPLEBAUM

The New New World Order

America and the New Geopolitics

IN THE EARLY 1990s, during the heady months that followed the collapse of the Berlin Wall, the world's diplomats, statesmen, and journalists competed to describe and define the shape of the new, post–Cold War world. The straightforward set of rules that had governed American foreign policy since the 1940s no longer applied. Our "friends" were no longer defined by their anticommunism, and our "enemies" were no longer defined by their affiliation with the Soviet Union. Many of the institutions created during the Cold War suddenly seemed irrelevant—NATO among them—and many of the specialists who had worked in these institutions suddenly found themselves at loose ends.

Some of the responses to the new situation were philosophical. Optimists like Frances Fukuyama claimed that we had reached the "End of History": liberal democracy and capitalism had triumphed, ideological struggle was over for good.

Pessimists like Samuel Huntington predicted the opposite: the onset of new "civilizational" wars between the West, Islam, and the Confucian world. Almost unnoticed, a very, very few people—oddballs like Gary Hart and Peggy Noonan—predicted that international terrorism would soon threaten American society, replacing the threat of nuclear war.

In the event, most of the institutional and political responses to the new situation had very little to do with any of these schools of thought. Instead, they developed *ad hoc*, in response to crises like the Iraqi invasion of Kuwait or the Balkan wars. If American policymakers had any philosophy at all, it was usually a rather superficial version of Fukuyama's optimism: the world is getting safer, and our job is to help it get safer faster. During what will now be remembered as the post–Cold War era—the long decade that stretched from November 1989 to September 2001—many practitioners of foreign policy did not think much about new threats that might face the United States. Instead, they argued about what it meant to conduct foreign policy in a world without any central threat at all.

As a result, there was no real organizing American diplomatic principle to speak of. True, George Bush Senior invented the phrase the "New World Order." But he had no policy to go with it: once the Gulf War ended, the coalition he had built to fight it quickly fell apart. Bill Clinton did have plenty of policies, but no philosophy with which to link them. "Nation-building" was the phrase sometimes used to talk about American policy in the Balkans and in Haiti. "Democracy-promotion" is perhaps more accurate. In practice, this meant that all around the world—in China, in Russia, in Malaysia, all over Africa, and above all in Serbia—the United States lectured and scolded and promoted its system, complaining about the closure of opposition newspapers, protesting the incarceration of opposition leaders. The State Department issued annual assessments of other countries' human rights records. NATO spent some of its time debating the pros and cons of enlargement, and even more of its time organizing peace-keeping operations in the Balkans. At the same time, more tasks were shifted onto the backs of multilateral institutions, the U.N. in particular, which were not prepared to shoulder the burdens of managing the world.

Some of these policies were not new. The United States had been promoting human rights abroad at least since the era of Jimmy Carter. In the past, however, democracy-promotion was part of the Cold War, and could be justified at home and abroad on those grounds. Promoting democracy for its own sake turned out to be more difficult, politically, than might have been expected. Professional diplomats hated it. One told me recently of the relief he feels, knowing he will no longer have to spend his days pushing American values down other peoples' unwilling throats. Congressmen hated it too, since they could never explain to their constituents where the American national interest lay in Kosovo. The business community couldn't understand why the oppression of Tibet need disrupt their trade with China. Ordinary Americans could never follow the intricacies of democracy-promotion, and have, as a result, consistently refused to read, think, or even speak about foreign affairs for the past decade.

But even human rights activists hated the inconsistencies of U.S. foreign policy. Everyone knew that the United States complained far more about the anti-democratic policies of indebted Kenya than it did about the far nastier anti-democratic policies of oil-rich Saudi Arabia. Everyone knew that the United States placed sanctions on India and Pakistan for possessing nuclear weapons, but not on Israel. Democracy-promotion pleased no one, not even those who spent all their time promoting it.

In retrospect, it is now clear that the high point, as well as the last hurrah, of the post–Cold War decade was the Community of Democracies conference. Organized under the patronage of then Secretary of State Madeleine Albright, it took place in Warsaw, in June 2000, and was attended by dozens of foreign ministers, from South Korea, from Benin, from Eastern and Western Europe. Her goal, Albright explained, was to persuade the world's democracies to start voting together and promoting their joint interests in international institutions, much as geographical caucuses do within the U.N. That sounded innocuous enough—but the conference was a flop. The meetings consisted of empty rhetorical exchanges. The conference statements were bland and predictable. In the planning stages, the delegates argued bitterly over who qualifies as a democracy, a question that was in the end resolved by American *diktat*, creating enormous resentments. The Russians refused to send a high-level representative; the Iranians were furious that they had been excluded. The conference received no media coverage whatsoever—at least until the French walked out. Refusing to sign the final declaration, the French foreign minister argued that the caucus would be nothing but another means for the United States to promote its interests abroad. Off the record, others agreed.

But the real trouble with Albright's ill-fated conference was the policy behind it. Democracy, it turned out, was too vague and ill-defined for diplomats and politicians to promote: it was like trying to promote "niceness," or "peace." All of which explains, in part, the breathtaking speed with which democracy-promotion is now being dismantled, and the mind-boggling rapidity with which the new paradigm, the War on Terrorism—the New New World Order—is now falling into place.

Clearly, the administration had more immediate concerns in the autumn of 2001—the war in Afghanistan, the international investigation of terrorist financing—but these will pale, in the long term, beside the foreign policy revolution which has only just begun.

THE BEGINNINGS OF A LONG WAR

To be fair, not all of the diplomatic changes that occurred in the autumn of 2001 are the direct result of the events of September 11. From the time of his election, George W. Bush's administration had a very different foreign policy agenda from that of its predecessors. More interested in self-defense, less interested in self-promotion, the new government had, by the autumn of 2001, already begun to prepare the American public and the rest of the world for a long debate about missile defense. In effect, the administration was already thinking about fighting terrorism, albeit a very specific, missile-guided sort of terrorism. This was not enough to prepare the United States for the attacks on New York and Washington, but it did mean that when the attacks occurred, the Bush administration was able to turn American foreign policy around very quickly. But the situation itself also made the government's task easier. Suddenly, the War on Terrorism, like the Cold War, provided the administration with both a practical and a philosophical guide to foreign policy, of a kind that the United States had not had since 1989.

Within days, the first building blocks of the New New World Order fell into place. Immediately, we had new allies, selected not for the quality of their free press but for the degree of cooperation they seemed likely to provide for the duration of what is going to be a long struggle against a new kind of enemy. Notably, they include Russia and China, two states with which we had previously been at odds. They also include

Russia's Central Asian satrapies, Tajikistan and Uzbekistan, both of whom have allowed us to use their territory for military purposes, something that was once unthinkable.

We also have new, more intense, and sometimes more complicated relationships with some of our older friends. Most obviously these include Western Europe and Israel (as I will explain in more depth), but there are others as well. Our relationships with India and Pakistan, for example, are suddenly both warmer and more difficult. Pakistan has already received huge injections of aid and support. During the war in Afghanistan, Pakistani officials worked more closely with their U.S. counterparts than they ever had in the past. At the same time, because there are strong links between al-Qaeda and Muslim separatists in Kashmir, the Indian government immediately offered its bases to the United States after September 11. As a result, when tensions between the two countries began to rise in the wake of a Kashmiri terrorist attack on the Indian parliament in December 2001, the United States found itself in an unfamiliar position. On the one hand, we were prisoners of our own rhetoric, bound to sympathize with the Indian victims of terror. On the other hand, we were in the unfamiliar position of dependence upon Pakistani troops, whose help we needed to patrol the Afghan-Pakistani border. In the past, we would have stayed as far away as possible from such a conflict. Now, we were drawn in, by both sides, by our own interests. It isn't impossible to imagine such a thing happening again, in north Africa, say, or the Middle East.

Our institutions are changing too. The purely theoretical and rather dull military debates of the past decade—along the lines of "should we be prepared to fight one large war or two small wars"—have suddenly given way to very concrete, very practical discussions about how to best defend Americans at home, and how to track down terrorists abroad. NATO has ceased to be a comfort club for Eastern European countries waiting to get into the European Union. Dusty, forgotten bits of the State Department—the Nuclear Non-Proliferation bureaucracy, for example—have already begun to receive more attention, more money, more influence, while others will be downgraded. Given the new terrorist threats to world leaders, for example, it would not be unreasonable to abandon the bloated, unnecessary, G7 summits altogether.

The role and relative importance of multilateral institutions has already changed too. In the aftermath of the terrorist attacks on New York and Washington, the American government instinctively looked not to the EU and the U.N., but to Britain's Prime Minister Blair, France's President Chirac and Prime Minister Jospin, Germany's Chancellor Schroeder. No one wanted to talk to Javier Solana, the EU's foreign policy spokesman. The U.N. Secretary-General, Kofi Annan, was hardly a major player in the first stages of the Afghan conflict either: when a real war needs to be fought, U.N. troops can't do it, and the EU's nonexistent army wasn't much help either. More broadly, all talk of a "post-patriotic" or a "post-nationalist" world—in which transnational institutions would gradually take over the management of the world's affairs—now seems redundant as well. In the wake of September 11, the nation-state suddenly looks like the only political institution capable of waging the long war against the terrorist threat.

These changes are permanent—although not everybody knows it yet. In the wake of the Taliban's collapse, many Americans began to relax, to hanker after a return to "normality" and the old days of "the economy, stupid." But it is too early to relax. The Taliban were toppled, but terrorism did not disappear along with them. Nor will it disappear, not in this generation, or even in the lifetime of anyone old enough to read this sentence. It has become clear, for starters, that Osama bin Laden's al-Qaeda is no small group of plotters, but rather a network of tens of thousands of trained fanatics, "spread throughout the world like time bombs, set to go off without warning," in the words of President Bush.

Nor is al-Qaeda likely to prove the last organization of its sort. The peculiar attributes of Western capitalism—its tendency to disrupt traditional ways of life, its materialism, its cosmopolitan nature—have produced enemies in the past. Parallels have been drawn between the Nazi cult of heroic sacrifice, Japanese kamikaze pilots—and the Afghan who told a British newspaper in the early days of the war that "Americans love Pepsi-Cola, but we love death." Capitalism, of which America has become the symbol, will also continue to produce enemies in the future, and they will not necessarily live in distant parts. Among the al-Qaeda prisoners whom the American army held captive in Guantanamo Bay were men from the Arab world, from Africa, from South Asia—and from Western Europe.

Indeed, the very existence of these Europeans, three Britons and up to seven Frenchmen, disproves the thesis that lay at the heart of democracy-promotion, the traditional thesis of benign global liberalism: that the more people of different cultures come into contact with one another, the more they will find common economic and other interests, and the more likely it is that they will remain at peace. These ten European terrorists were not just similar to us: they *were* us. Just like the al-Qaeda activists who started dreaming of destroying the World Trade Center from their universities in Hamburg, the ten Europeans in U.S. captivity chose to fight the West not because they were ignorant of the West, but because they knew it all too well.

If, in the future, others of their ilk choose to keep up that fight, the technology is already available. By this, I don't mean that al-Qaeda's plans to make chemical weapons were probably already well advanced, or that nuclear technology is now readily available, although all of that is true. I mean, rather, that the attacks of September 11 were not the result of recent advances in fiber optics or information technology: it has been possible to use an airplane to hit a large building for the better part of a century. The explosives that suicide bombers are using to terrorize West Jerusalem aren't exactly of recent invention either. While the latter don't necessarily kill vast numbers of people, they've seriously damaged the Israeli economy, not to mention the Israeli psyche, shaping Israeli politics and security policy for years to come. Any group of ideologically driven people could, with sufficient numbers, achieve the same in New York City—starting tomorrow.

Debate about whether all this is good or bad will, of course, continue. Writing in the online journal *Slate*, for example, William Saletan pointed out that maintaining close relationships with unpleasant regimes will ultimately cast doubt upon our claim to be fighting against terrorists, and in favor of "progress and pluralism," just as they once cast doubt on our claims to be promoting democracy. Others, by contrast, have rejoiced in the end of democracy-promotion. "We cannot re-engineer other societies, and we risk enormous resentment when we try," wrote Claudia Rosett in the *Wall Street Journal*.

Much of the general public, however, is likely to approve of the new foreign policy. Like the Cold War, the War on Terrorism appeases the idealism of Americans: we are, after all, fighting to rid the world of an evil. But it also appeals to our realism. No intellectual contortions are required to explain why the fight against Osama bin Laden is well within the sphere of America's national interest. At least for the moment, the "body-bag syndrome"—America's inclination to retreat rapidly from any conflict that might actually kill an American—has vanished.

NEW COMPLICATIONS AND
OLD STICKING POINTS

But although the logic of the War on Terrorism is straightforward, the events of September 11 have not suddenly made the world into a simple place. One of the dangers of the New New World Order is that it appears, like the Cold War, to make the world appear less complicated than it actually is. They may seem straightforward, but all of our new policies, our new friendships, and our new enemies bring with them new dangers. To counter them, we will need to think very creatively indeed. After a decade in which foreign policy was considered virtually irrelevant—a decade in which the CIA virtually failed to hire any Arabic speakers—there is no guarantee that our foreign policy establishment will rise to the task.

Oddly, it is our friendships, both new and old, that may cause us some of the most formidable problems. As I say, this is going to be a long war. While it is being fought, we will need allies, and some of them will seem very strange. As was the case during the Cold War, we have already begun relationships with countries whose political systems are radically different, even inimical to ours. Our new contacts with Uzbekistan and Tajikistan, for example, are unlikely to prove mere alliances of convenience: although the war in Afghanistan proved short, the country still needs to rebuild itself. For that, its neighbors may have to be roped in to help. Yet at the same time, in a world of instant communications and satellite television, it is no longer possible for anyone to hide the differences between our system of government and the Uzbek system. Countries cannot be isolated from the world now, as they could be twenty or thirty years ago. Differences will be exposed, and they will matter. This caution applies to Tajikistan and Uzbekistan, as well as to Iran and Pakistan. It also applies, albeit atypically and idio-syncratically, to Russia.

One of the great surprises of the terrorist attacks of September 11 was the instant, dramatic, and profound impact they clearly made upon the Russian president, Vladimir Putin. He not only announced his support for any American retaliation, he made an essential material contribution as well, offering the United States use of Russian-controlled bases in Central Asia, as well as access to Russian intelligence sources in Afghanistan. These decisions were clearly Putin's, and Putin's alone. The Russian population's support for the American War on Terrorism is lukewarm. The Russian security establishment remains largely opposed to the United States, as it always has been, and some of its members are clearly agitated by Putin's policy.

Yet Putin's decisions were not taken out of admiration for President Bush or fondness for America either. As a friend of mine in Moscow put it, "The events of September 11 were so advantageous to the Russian government, you might think they flew the airplanes themselves." While one might not want to take counterintuitive conspiracy theories that far, it is true that a number of Russia's more ambitious foreign policy goals do suddenly appear within reach. Since the collapse of the Soviet Union, Russia has been looking for an international role, preferably to be played on an equal footing with the United States. Overnight, a role has defined itself: Russia will be America's partner in the international fight against terrorism. As a result, American criticism of Chechnya will soften, and has done so already. Neither the creation of a missile defense system nor NATO expansion will grind to a permanent halt, but both will now take place only after extensive official consultations with Russia. At a post–September 11 meeting with Lord Robertson, the secretary-general of NATO, Putin seemed to give his blessing to the idea of expansion. What he appears to want, above all, is for NATO to ask politely for his stamp of approval.

On the face of things, this looks like a success: for the past ten years, successive U.S. administrations have tried to lure Russia into international institutions, to tempt it into becoming an "ordinary" power instead of a rogue state. Overnight, that's exactly what's happened. Russia seems eager to play our game, join our institutions, help fight our war. And yet—there is still no evidence that either Russia's economy or Russia's system of values has come any closer to ours. Our new relationship appears to depend largely on the attitude of the president, and does not yet reflect a deeper Russian-American kinship. Down the line, Russia's mixed motives may even bring us trouble. It will, for example, be difficult for President Bush to maintain that this is not a war against Islam, if one of his most important allies believes that this *is* a war against Islam. Russia's behavior in Chechnya will invariably embarrass us too. Putin may believe that he is fighting terrorists, but Russian soldiers believe they are fighting the Chechen nation. Civilian casualties are common, the destruction of property is widespread. How will we explain our silence on Chechnya to the Islamic members of our anti-terrorist coalition?

But then, down the line, some of our other, closer, older allies may bring us trouble as well, as a wide range of conflicting currents strain the trans-Atlantic relationship. Our own feelings about Europe appear, at the moment, decidedly mixed. On the one hand, we did not need Europe's military assistance in Afghanistan at all. On the contrary, some have begun to wonder whether Europe's military weakness, caused by decades of underinvestment and poor leadership, will not make European soldiers an actual liability in future conflicts.

On the other hand, we still need European allies in other ways, and will go on needing them in the future. We need them to help in tracking the flows of terrorist money, as well as in capturing and deporting the terrorists themselves, many of whom are based in Europe. We need European help in rebuilding Afghanistan. We may also need European moral and logistical support in any future war in Iraq or North Korea. Further down the line, we will need European support in promoting our vision of global capitalism and international free trade.

But if we are ambivalent about Europe, it is no less ambivalent about us. True, government leaders and the European public immediately expressed horror and sympathy in the wake of September 11. Over subsequent weeks, however, the European media expressed a good deal less solidarity. The *New Statesman*, an influential, pro-Blair, moderately left-wing British journal, opined that "Americans would do well to ask themselves why, despite what should be an enormous propaganda advantage in beaming their way of life to every corner of the globe, their ideals and values have signally failed to inspire the Third World young in the way that Marxism did and Islam now does," and even laid some of the blame for the events on the American voters who had the gall to choose George Bush over Al Gore and Ralph Nader. Similar views appeared in the French, Spanish, and Italian press.

These were not majority sentiments to begin with, but they are slowly gaining currency among European politicians, building on a fundamental anti-Americanism that has never really disappeared. As a result, there were first a few small incidents, lukewarm words from the French prime minister, Lionel Jospin, stonewalling from Belgian police who were asked to help share information with Americans investigating al-Qaeda. Resentment of perceived American unilateralism then burst into the open following the publication of photographs of America's al-Qaeda prisoners in Guantanamo Bay, and the news that the United States did not intend to abide by the Geneva Convention on POWs in its treatment of them. American carelessness was partly responsible: as it turned out, there was no reason for the United States not to hold a tribunal, declare the prisoners "unlawful combatants"—which they were—abide by the Convention and be done with it. But the anger was magnified, both by resentment and by partisan politics. It was not accidental that the loudest criticism of the Republican administration came from the more left-leaning members of the European press, and from the left-wing political leaders who now run most of Western Europe.

Paradoxically, the strongest American ally in Europe is in some ways the most potentially ambivalent of all. Since the afternoon of September 11, when he spoke of Britain standing "shoulder to shoulder" with America, British Prime Minister Tony Blair has taken on the role of America's greatest ally. Yet Blair is not supporting the United States, as many Americans believe, merely out of loyalty to the United States or to the old Anglo-American special relationship. What motivates Blair is something different: his semi-mystical, quasi-religious, and rather ill-defined belief in the unique possibilities of international cooperation. It isn't a consistent position—he has been notably uninterested in involving the European Union in the anti-terrorist effort—but it is deeply felt nevertheless. "There's a coming together," he said in a speech he made to his party soon after September 11: "The power of community is asserting itself. I have long believed this interdependence defines the new world we live in. We can't do it all. Neither can the Americans. But the power of the international community could, together, if it chose to."

While Blair's deep devotion to an almost nineteenth-century form of international idealism doesn't necessarily weaken the British-American alliance, it does mean that he, like other Europeans, has an agenda that Americans don't have. He is a devotee of the international legal system—he was one of the first critics of the American prison camp in Guantanamo Bay—and may perhaps decide it needs louder defending. Or perhaps he'll decide, at some later date, that U.S. policy in Afghanistan—or Iraq—is not contributing as much to the growth of "interdependence" as he thought it would. Because Blair is fighting this war for his own reasons, and not for America's reasons, he may be less than enthusiastic if it takes a direction that doesn't suit his vision. At some point we may all find out that we are not quite such good friends as we thought.

But then, the complications that could arise from our relationship with some other long-time American allies—the Israelis—are much greater. In the immediate aftermath of the September 11 attacks, Ariel Sharon, the Israeli prime minister, drew the parallel between Palestinian terrorism and the terrorism of Osama bin Laden very bluntly: "Arafat is our bin Laden," he said on the day of the attacks. A series of suicide attacks in Israel in the weeks that followed the U.S. attacks confirmed this sense, at least within Israel and the United States, and it is unlikely to go away. In his State of the Union address, President Bush himself specifically placed Hamas and Hezbollah, both active in Israel, both quietly tolerated by Arafat, among the terrorist groups whose training centers the United States must destroy. As I write this, it seems only a matter of time before the United States cuts off Arafat for good—a position unthinkable before September 11.

Outside the United States, the mood is quite different. Internationally, Arafat is hardly an admired figure. Yet neither he, nor the terrorists he tolerates, are perceived to be the sole cause of the Middle Eastern conflict either. Many in Europe believe that Israel's occupation of the West Bank in general, and the Israeli settlement policy in particular, are also responsible for continuing strife in the region. Many Israelis believe the same: some in the Israeli army have even begun to argue that the occupation of the West Bank is corrupting Israel's own soldiers. This rapidly growing gap in perceptions of the Middle East leaves an open field for diplomatic, ideological, and military conflicts and misunderstandings of all kinds. If the United States wholeheartedly identifies itself with Israel, it risks being perceived around the world as the enforcer of a "colonial" regime. On the other hand, if the United States is engaged in a war on international terrorism, how can it make exceptions for the suicide bombers of West Jerusalem?

Although these issues are thrown into particularly sharp contrast by the harsh realities of the Middle East, they could emerge elsewhere too. Wherever we choose to fight terrorism— whether in Israel, in the Philippines, in Colombia, in Northern Ireland—we will also be drawn into local conflicts that have their own history, their own dynamic, their own logic. In Afghanistan, we were able to engage in a "neutral" war against what was clearly a terrorist regime. In future, we may start out a military engagement intending only to fight terrorism—and rapidly discover that our mere presence implicates us in whole welter of other, unwanted issues. Over the coming months and years, it is not only our friends who will confuse us. On the contrary, I have left the subject of "our new enemies" for the end because it is in some senses the most difficult of all.

OUR NEW ENEMIES

The problem is evident from the confusion over the definition of the enemy itself. We are fighting terrorists—but which ones? George Bush has spoken of a war against "terrorism with a global reach." I assume that means "terrorism that can reach the territory of the United States." He has also, as I say, mentioned Hezbollah and Hamas, although not yet the Basque separatists, the Tamil Tigers, or the IRA. But why the distinction? And what if it turns out (as it has already) that the terrorists we are fighting have made common cause with some of the terrorists we are not fighting? Al-Qaeda has almost certainly funded indigenous terrorist groups in Kashmir, and this has already led us into involvement in some tricky negotiations in South Asia. Al-Qaeda has also funded indigenous terrorist groups in China: down the line, that may put us in the very strange position of aiding the Chinese government as well.

Confusion will also result from the difficulty of isolating terrorism from other international scourges. We are fighting terrorists—but how do we fight an enemy that has no army? In the case of Afghanistan, a military option was available—thanks to the Northern Alliance's eagerness to cooperate. The same could prove true in the nations President Bush has also identified as the "Axis of Evil," Iran, Iraq, and North Korea. When planes and bombs can be used against such countries, they should be used, not only because they work but because they will deter others.

Completely different, however, and far more difficult, will be the war against terrorists who live and operate in countries we cannot bomb, such as Britain and France. In the modern world, terrorism has the same organic relationship with organized crime that communism had with the secret police. Terrorists make use of the same shell companies, the same offshore accounts, and the same money-laundering operations as the Colombian drug kings and the Italian mafia, surviving not within states but on their fringes. Unraveling all that will also involve us in the financial affairs of many other nations, as it already has done. Dozens of banks and financial and government institutions have already been involved in the hunt for al-Qaeda funding, sometimes in strange combinations. In the wake of September 11, an Indian banker of my acquaintance, working for a branch of an American bank in Warsaw, spent several days trolling his accounts for evidence of terrorist activity. He did so because his company requested it. If his bosses did not happen to be American, would we be able to count on his participation?

The nature of our new opponents means we need to start thinking—now—about new ways to fight them. By itself, unilateral military activity will not be enough, although I realize that some now believe otherwise. By acting decisively in Afghanistan, the argument goes, President Bush has made unilateralism work for the United States. If our allies don't like it, we don't care. If our opponents don't like it, let them fight harder.

In fact, this argument draws the wrong lessons from our military success in Afghanistan. That war was won thanks in part—but only in part—to the overwhelming military might of the United States. Without the cooperation of other countries, notably Russia and Pakistan, we would not have been able to exercise that military might to such good effect. Without allies among the Afghan Northern Alliance and some Pashtun groups, we would at the very least have faced much higher U.S. casualties. In fact, the war was a diplomatic and intelligence success as much as it was a military success.

Over the coming decades, we need to develop the same mix of policies to deal with the wide mix of threats we now face. What we need is not arrogant unilateralism, in other words, but intelligent unilateralism. Intelligent unilateralism means that we do not deliberately antagonize friends, or start unnecessary conflicts. Intelligent unilateralism also means that we relearn the importance of selling ourselves abroad, both to our allies and to our enemies. Our long-term security now depends directly not just on our ability to develop and pay for better weapons but on our ability to organize our friends and manipulate our enemies, on our diplomacy, and on our judicious rather than our overwhelming use of military force.

Intelligent unilateralism will also require us to become interested in a whole host of issues that we have hitherto ignored. Over time, I predict we will ourselves be interested not only in other peoples' nuclear programs but in their immigration and asylum policies; in their police forces; and above all in their education systems. The Taliban, after all, were the product of the Pakistani *madrassahs*. If we want postwar Afghanistan to be a moderate Islamic state, we may have to interest ourselves in what children learn in Afghan schools. Our failure to interest ourselves in what was taught in Saudi schools may well help explain the growth of al-Qaeda itself.

Of course, by "interesting ourselves in others' policies" I do not mean that we should simply continue our old methods of democracy-promotion, with added bells and whistles. American involvement abroad can no longer be perceived as a form of do-goodism or charity, which everyone in the United States feels to be unnecessary and everyone outside the United States finds to be hypocritical. In the new era, we are no longer selling democracy for its own sake, but exporting security, both for our sake and for the sake of other potential victims. We aren't counting independent newspapers, we are—or should be—trying to ensure that Saudi children do not grow up believing that the United States is solely responsible for their economic failure and intellectual frustration. The president himself has called for a "new effort to encourage development and education and opportunity in the Islamic world," and the administration has quietly pledged millions of dollars to fund education in Afghanistan.

To carry out an intelligent unilateralist policy, what we also need is not merely better weapons but better intelligence operatives, ones who are capable of working with local people.

We also need better ways of speaking to foreigners. The old, outmoded, or defunct institutions—Radio Free Europe, USIA—would be insufficient in a world where the most influential medium is satellite television, even if they still functioned as they once did. During the Afghan war, U.S. officials initially refused to appear on Al-Jazeera, the Arabic-language satellite television station. A few weeks after the bombardment began, however, they changed their policy, and rightly so: the appearance of American diplomats, speaking fluent, classical Arabic, apparently marked a turning point in Arab perceptions of the war.

Still, a few Arabic-speaking officials are unlikely to change the hearts and minds of a generation. If the launch of the Soviet Union's first satellite convinced the American government to begin promoting the teaching of science and math, the events of September 11 should now convince the American government of the need to promote the teaching of languages and history, especially those of the "exotic" peoples and nations of which we know little. And not just the government: The education of Americans for the new era is a matter for individuals, for universities, and above all for our provincial and insular media.

The choice is a stark one: If we do not learn better ways of dealing with the outside world, then the outside world will, once again, come to us.

BYRON YORK

The World That
Didn't Change—Much

Partisanship and the
Politics of National
Security After 9/11

NOT LONG AFTER the terrorist attacks in New York and Washington, Democratic strategists James Carville, Stanley Greenberg, and Robert Shrum convened a series of focus groups to gauge the political impact of September 11. What did it mean for Democrats who had planned a fall battle with President George W. Bush over the economy, health care, and the environment? What did it mean for Bush himself? And what about congressional Republicans? Two weeks after the attacks, the strategists' group, Democracy Corps, met with voters in Milwaukee, Tampa, Atlanta, and Philadelphia. The next week, the pollsters ran focus groups in Toledo, Ohio, and Runnemede, New Jersey, followed by Oakland, Albuquerque, Seattle, and Des Moines. To supplement their findings, the researchers also conducted a nationwide poll on the same questions.

The team came away with the conclusion that 9/11 "created

a new period which is, in many ways, radically different from what has gone before." Democrats, they stressed, not only had to support a popular Republican president on war and security issues, they also had to "adopt a tone consistent with the seriousness of this moment" and stay away from "partisan-sounding attacks." Yet after that warning, Carville, Greenberg, and Shrum went on to outline a political strategy that was remarkably similar to what Democrats had planned prior to September 11. "We have looked closely at the national survey and focus groups," they wrote, "and we believe this is a moment of opportunity for Democrats." The research, they concluded, suggested that Democrats could safely and profitably attack the president on . . . the economy, health care, and the environment.

A few months later, on Friday, January 4, 2002, Senate Majority Leader Tom Daschle delivered a major policy address in which he laid out some of the Democratic Party's themes for the midterm election year (and made what was possibly the opening statement of a 2004 Daschle presidential campaign). "Our nation is engaged in two great battles," Daschle said. "In the first battle, the battle against terrorism, President Bush and his national security team are doing a superb job." But in the second, which Daschle called "the battle to deal with the economic challenges facing our nation," Daschle said Bush and the Republican Party had brought about "the most dramatic fiscal deterioration in our nation's history." While the administration blamed the terrorist attacks for the disappearance of the once-healthy budget surplus, Daschle strongly disagreed. "September 11th and the war aren't the only reasons the surplus is nearly gone," he said (it would later disappear altogether). "They're not even the biggest reasons. The biggest reason is the tax cut." The speech—which sounded as if it had been written by the team at Democracy Corps—was the highest-profile political attack on the president since the terrorist attacks.

Daschle's words set off a spate of articles about the re-emergence of partisanship in Washington; the front page of the *Washington Post* declared flatly, "Partisan Politics Returns to Capital." But the fact that Carville, Greenberg, and Shrum began their strategizing before the dust from the terrorist attacks had even settled suggests that partisan maneuvering never went away, not even in the immediate shock of September 11. (There was no comparable Republican polling going on in that period, although GOP strategists kept close tabs on a variety of media polls showing Bush with sky-high job approval ratings.) Rather than entirely suppress their partisan instincts, Democratic and Republican leaders, as they mapped the post–September 11 landscape, realized they would have to adjust their stands on some issues if they were to remain politically viable in the weeks after the terrorist attacks. In some cases, Democrats had to retreat, at least temporarily, from long-held positions on civil liberties. In other cases, Republicans had to retreat, also temporarily, from equally long-held desires to limit the size and scope of government. Yet in other cases not dealing directly with security issues, such as debates on tax cuts and health care, neither side felt the need to depart from traditional party doctrine.

That pattern of selective restrategizing emerges from a review of the three most important pieces of legislation to result from the terrorist attacks: the Uniting and Strengthening America by Providing Appropriate Tools Required to Intercept and Obstruct Terrorism Act (the strained acronym now known as the USA Patriot Act); the Aviation and Transportation Security Act; and the failed economic stimulus bill. In the debate over the USA Patriot Act, mainstream Democrats, aware of polls showing strong public support for greater federal law enforcement powers, stifled some of their objections to the Bush Justice Department's request for unprecedented surveillance authority. In the Aviation and Transportation Security Act debate, some Republicans, watching polls that showed the public in favor of federalizing baggage screeners at airports nationwide, held in check their instinctive objections to the prospect of adding 28,000 workers to the government payroll. But in the economic stimulus fight, both parties stuck to their guns in a battle over tax cuts that was remarkably similar to the debate that took place in the winter and spring of 2001, long before planes crashed into the World Trade Center and the Pentagon.

Throughout, party leaders compromised when necessary—avoiding "partisan-sounding attacks"—while making sure to give as little ground as possible. And in the end, bills that were urgently needed to improve the United States' ability to protect against future attacks—the anti-terrorism measure and the aviation security bill—were passed, while a bill that was not at all necessary—the stimulus package—failed. Contrary to the contemporary conventional wisdom that the emergence of partisanship might undermine the nation's response to terrorism, each side's partisan calculations in fact played a positive role in the process, helping pass the best proposals and kill the worst ones.

THE USA PATRIOT ACT

The ease with which the September 11 plotters made their way around the United States—exploiting weaknesses in the immigration system, obtaining drivers' licenses and other identification, and moving freely past airport security checkpoints—highlighted dozens of problems the government faced in trying to prevent future acts of terrorism. To make matters worse, it was never clear from the first days after the attacks whether there were more al-Qaeda cells operating in the United States. Given that danger, making sure that no co-conspirators in the September 11 attacks remained at large, tracking down other terrorist groups, and strengthening existing law enforcement authority became top domestic priorities of the Bush administration.

On September 19, Attorney General John Ashcroft presented Congress with a list of proposals the administration wanted to incorporate into a new anti-terrorism bill. The administration wanted expanded powers of surveillance under the Foreign Intelligence Security Act, including greater wiretap and call-tracing authority as well as increased ability to monitor e-mails and Internet use. Ashcroft also wanted to allow law enforcement and intelligence agencies to share information in terrorist investigations, something that had not been done in the past. And he wanted to give prosecutors the power to detain suspects for extended periods of time without filing formal charges against them.

All were powers that law enforcement had sought at various times in the past, although never in the context of a national emergency. On the question of wiretaps, for example, prosecutors had long chafed at having to obtain court orders that applied only to a particular telephone a suspect might use—a practice made obsolete by criminals' increasing use of multiple cell phones. After September 11, the Bush administration simply revived a long-time law enforcement request for so-called "roving" wiretap authority, which would allow investigators to obtain a single court order to eavesdrop on all of a suspect's telephone communications, no matter how many different telephones were involved.

Other items on the law enforcement wish-list that the administration included in the anti-terrorism bill were new rules covering "pen register" and "trap and trace" technologies. A pen register is a device that records the phone numbers of calls made from a particular telephone. A trap and trace device records the numbers of calls coming into a particular telephone. Law enforcement officers, who are required to obtain a judge's warrant to tap a telephone, were held to a lower, but still burdensome, standard to use pen register and trap and trace; in the terrorism bill, the administration wanted virtually unlimited freedom to use them.

The Justice Department also asked for greater authority to monitor Internet traffic. In recent years, law enforcement officials had become increasingly worried about the criminal potential of a technology called "stegonagraphy," which involves coding hidden messages inside seemingly innocent-looking materials on the Net. Some investigators believe stegonagraphy could be used by terrorists to transmit detailed instructions, building plans, financial documents, or other information in connection with a planned attack. The administration wanted more freedom to use existing surveillance technology—known as "Carnivore"—and hoped the terrorism emergency would overcome previous congressional doubts about its widespread use.

Beyond technological advances, the Justice Department also wanted to knock down a legal barrier that had in the past impeded terrorist investigations. In post–September 11 reviews of America's response to terrorism, the Clinton administration came under heavy criticism for having relied on law enforcement rather than aggressive intelligence and military operations to find and destroy terrorist cells. In particular, the former president was criticized for assigning the investigation of the 1993 World Trade Center bombing exclusively to the Justice Department, effectively shutting out the government's intelligence agencies. The problem was that prosecutors used a grand jury to conduct much of the bombing investigation, meaning that whatever was learned through the grand jury had to remain a closely held secret under Rule 6(e) of the Federal Rules of Criminal Procedure. The rule forbade prosecutors from sharing grand jury information with outsiders, including government intelligence experts who had spent years keeping tabs on international terrorists. During the bombing investigation, then-CIA director James Woolsey became increasingly frustrated at the secretiveness of Justice Department prosecutors. "Nobody outside the prosecutorial team and maybe the FBI had access [to evidence in the case]," Woolsey said later, "because it was all under grand jury secrecy." The Bush proposal called for law enforcement and intelligence agencies to be allowed to share information in future terrorist investigations.

Finally, the administration wanted the ability to arrest and hold terrorist suspects at length without formally charging them with crimes. In the days after September 11, federal officials held hundreds of people for varying periods of time as investigators determined whether they were connected to the terrorist attacks. Some were charged with federal crimes. A few were held as material witnesses. And most were held, and ultimately charged, on immigration violations. In nearly all those cases, the suspects were charged within days, but some detainees were held more than a week, and sometimes longer, before facing formal charges.

Many of the administration's requests—wiretaps, Internet surveillance, evidence sharing, expanded detentions, as well as greater authority to track financial transactions—were proposals that had sparked determined opposition in the past, much of it from Democrats, but also from civil liberties–minded Republicans. It's safe to say that without the events of September 11, the administration would never have succeeded in winning congressional approval for any of them. Several of the president's requests raised genuine civil liberties issues, and not only the fringes of both parties but many in the mainstream might have opposed them under different circumstances. But September 11 made it virtually impossible for mainstream officials of either party to reject the administration's proposals, effectively banishing opposition to the political fringes.

On the left, there were a few liberals, like California Democratic Rep. Maxine Waters, who worried that racial and ethnic minorities would be targeted by newly empowered law enforcement under the guise of the war against terrorism. "We cannot be rushed into allowing this tragic moment to cause us to support a violation of privacy or the Constitution," Waters said at the first public hearing on the issue, on September 24. On the right, there was the conservative Georgia Republican Rep. Bob Barr, who had long questioned the government's expanding powers of surveillance. "Why is it necessary to rush this through?" Barr asked at the same hearing. "Does it have anything to do with the fact that the department has sought many of these authorities on numerous other occasions, has been unsuccessful in obtaining them, and now seeks to take advantage of what is obviously an emergency situation to obtain authorities that it has been unable to obtain previously?"

But Waters and Barr had few supporters. In part that was because some left- and right-leaning politicians who might normally have opposed the administration's request sincerely believed that circumstances called for extraordinary measures. But other potential opponents were undoubtedly swayed by the extraordinary popularity of President George W. Bush and his anti-terrorism policies.

The attacks had an astonishing effect on the president's job approval rating. In a poll taken immediately before September 11, the Gallup organization found the president's job approval rating to be just 51 percent, with 39 percent disapproval. In a poll taken on September 21 and 22, immediately after Bush's tremendously well received address to both houses of Congress, Gallup found the president's approval rating to be 90 percent, with 6 percent disapproval. The next month, it stayed in the same range, as it did in November and December—an unprecedented length of time for any president to enjoy such popularity. Few Republicans, no matter how deep their opposition to government surveillance powers, would want to take a stand against those numbers. The same was true for Democrats, who also saw that some of their key constituent groups, which might normally be counted on to oppose almost anything George W. Bush did, instead gave the president relatively high ratings. In early October, for example, Gallup found that 68 percent of black Americans gave Bush a positive job approval rating.

Polls like that made it impossible for the president's opponents, even if they were so inclined, to gain any traction against him on the terrorism issue. So even though there were isolated complaints about the administration's proposals—Democratic Sen. Patrick Leahy publicly fretted that "if the Constitution is shredded, the terrorists win"—the anti-terrorism bill raced through Congress. Both houses put it on a fast track that limited debate and streamlined normal parliamentary measures. In the end, the bill passed by a margin of 356 to 66 in the House and 98 to 1 in the Senate (Wisconsin Democrat Russell Feingold was the lone dissenter).

The president won approval for nearly everything he wanted. "We're dealing with terrorists who operate by highly sophisticated methods and technologies, some of which were not even available when our existing laws were written," Bush said when he signed the bill into law on October 26. "The bill before me takes into account the new realities and dangers posed by modern terrorists." Leahy and other Democrats in the audience could only look on and applaud.

THE AVIATION SECURITY ACT

After the search for terrorists, the government's second major domestic priority was reform of the airport security system. There was no doubt from the moment of the attacks that an aviation-security bill would be part of Congress' anti-terrorist agenda. But what should be done?

The Senate took the early lead on the issue, and its first efforts were strikingly limited. Since the September 11 hijackers had used knives and box cutters to subdue passengers and then break into the cockpit, lawmakers immediately moved to ban knives and box cutters and make cockpit doors stronger. Beyond that, the Senate proposed expanding the nearly moribund sky marshal system, requiring an increased number of marshals on domestic flights. Finally, the Senate wanted to federalize the 28,000 baggage screeners who work at security checkpoints in airports across the country. Under the Senate plan, they would work under the supervision of the Justice Department, which would be given control of aviation security nationwide.

The Senate raced to finish work on the bill by October 11 (lawmakers were anxious to make news by taking tough action on the one-month anniversary of the terrorist attacks). But as they considered the bill's provisions, Republican senators were perplexed. Was it a good idea for the Justice Department to handle airport security? Would the Transportation Department be better? Should baggage screeners be federal employees? Would it be better if they were private contractors working under strict federal supervision?

In such a situation, Republican senators would normally look to the White House for guidance, but in the early days of the aviation security bill, the White House was virtually silent. Without leadership from George W. Bush, most senators paid careful attention to polls gauging public opinion on the air safety issue. For example, a Gallup survey found that 96 percent of Americans polled favored strengthening cockpit doors, 90 percent supported expanding the sky marshal program, and, in what would become the key issue in the debate over air security, 77 percent supported a full federal takeover of baggage screening.

As the bill moved through the Senate, some conservative Republicans privately conceded that, despite the poll numbers, they had deep reservations about federalizing the screeners. Indeed, there were good reasons to doubt the Senate plan. Everyone knew how hard it was to fire a federal employee for sub-par performance; polls showed that even federal workers themselves believed the government placed too little emphasis on worker accountability. Republican senators also doubted that simply making the screeners federal workers would make them more effective or reliable than private screeners working under close government supervision. And some Republicans opposed on general principles the idea of adding 28,000 new workers to the federal payroll.

But Democrats, buoyed by that 77 percent approval figure, strongly pressed what they said was the urgent need to federalize the screeners. The White House remained silent. After a brief debate, Republican senators saw that there was nothing to gain by voting against an airline security bill that enjoyed clear popular support. The bill passed the Senate 100 to 0.

At the same time, doubts about the wisdom of the Senate's approach were growing in the House. As the Senate rushed forward, several members in the House were actually studying the aviation security issue in far more detail than anyone had done in the Senate. House researchers decided it would be better to place aviation security in the hands of the Transportation Department (it would have been enormously burdensome to the Justice Department). They came up with new suggestions to increase security all around airports—ground crew areas, baggage areas, etc.—and not just in cockpits. And they took a close look at the question of federalizing baggage screeners. After studying airport security systems in Israel and Europe, they concluded that the world's most effective systems relied on private screeners. And that is what they wrote into the final Republican House bill.

As a vote neared in the House, President Bush finally took a position on the issue, coming out strongly for the Republican plan. But most House Democrats supported the full-federalization Senate bill, and it was not clear which would prevail in the House, where the Republican majority was very thin. When time came to vote, Democrats tried to substitute the full-federalization Senate bill for the private-screener House measure. The vote was nearly as close as it could possibly be, with Republicans defeating the Senate bill by 218 to 214. Later, when the GOP version came up for a vote, it passed easily, 286 to 139. (After the Democratic measure was defeated, dozens of Democrats—69 in all—turned around and voted for the Republican bill, suggesting that they were prepared to vote for almost any type of aviation security bill.)

Even though the Republican version passed the House, it faced a difficult fight in the conference committee that would reconcile it with the Senate bill. Everyone knew the GOP had narrowly prevailed in the House, while the Senate measure passed 100 to 0. If every single senator, from Jesse Helms to Barbara Boxer, supported full federalization, why shouldn't that be the version that became law?

As the conference began, some GOP senators tried to influence the negotiations by declaring that they were having second thoughts about their votes in favor of a fully federalized screening force. "While we supported and the Senate unanimously passed S. 1447 [the Aviation Security Act], we had strong misgivings with respect to the federalization of airport screeners," a group of seventeen Republicans wrote in a letter to the chairmen of the Senate Commerce Committee and the House Transportation Committee. "In addition to the urgency of passing an aviation security bill, our support of S. 1447 was largely due to other important security provisions such as reinforced cockpit doors and an increased presence of federal air marshals." The letter was signed by some of the Senate's most conservative members, including Jesse Helms, Mitch McConnell, Don Nickles, and Phil Gramm.

But it was far too late for second thoughts. By the time the conference committee convened, Republicans knew the public still firmly supported federal screeners. Conservative lawmakers saw little benefit—and much peril—in holding up the final passage of an aviation security bill over the issue. What if there was another airline terrorist attack while they were dickering over public vs. private baggage screeners? That would be nothing short of political disaster. So even though some GOP lawmakers strongly believed that private screeners would make the system safer than government screeners, they went along with the Senate. The president did, too, signing the Aviation and Transportation Security Act into law on November 19. "The broad support for this bill shows that our country is united in this crisis," the president said during a signing ceremony held at Reagan National Airport. "We have our political differences, but we're united to defend our country, and we're united to protect our people."

THE STIMULUS BILL

Both the anti-terrorism bill and the aviation security bill touched on issues that had deep emotional resonance with a public that remained terrified of a new terrorist attack in the days after September 11. Americans wanted government to take action. But the third major issue taken up by Congress in the post–September 11 period, the economic stimulus bill, touched on no such raw nerves. Yes, the country suffered economically from the terrorist attacks. But there was no clear consensus on what, if anything, the federal government should do about it.

The attacks came at a time when the raging question on Capitol Hill was whether the government should spend the estimated $157 billion budget surplus—made up almost entirely of excess Social Security funds—on paying down the national debt, or whether some of the money should be used for other purposes. Democrats favored the former, while the Bush White House, struggling to reconcile its spending priorities with the president's tax cut, began making the case that the Social Security surplus could be used for general spending under certain circumstances. On August 24, the president said, "I've said that the only reason we should use Social Security funds is in case of an economic recession or war." At the time, of course, Bush thought he was making the case for increased spending in an economic downturn, but by September 11, he had both a recession *and* a war. And on that day, the debate over how to spend the surplus simply vanished. There was no question that the Social Security surplus—plus a good deal more—would be spent on strengthening security, helping New York and Washington recover, and launching a worldwide war against Osama bin Laden and other terrorists.

Immediately after the attacks, the administration asked Congress for $20 billion in supplemental spending authority. Lawmakers, not wanting to fall behind in the race to help the American people, quickly passed a bill providing for *$40* billion. The first half of the money would be spent immediately, as the president proposed, and the second half would be worked out later.

Although the money was intended for anti-terrorism and relief work, the new spending authority had the practical effect of freeing up existing funds for spending on all varieties of things not related to terrorism. For example, before the attacks President Bush had requested $18 billion for defense spending above what was in the budget resolution at that time. The move faced stiff opposition from many Democrats, who wanted to use part of that money for education and other nondefense purposes. The two sides were headed for a big fight, but after September 11 lawmakers realized they could take some of the defense money and use it for education, and make up the defense portion—and more—from the supplemental spending bill. The problem was solved, and a political battle was averted.

That wasn't the only example. Indeed, lawmakers seized on the national emergency as a rationale for all sorts of other nonemergency spending. Existing spending projects were recast as urgent national security issues. Isn't transportation a national security issue? Why not spend more on highways? How about water projects? And what about food? One lawmaker championed a proposed $3.5 billion peanut subsidy on the grounds that it would strengthen national security. Although there were some voices of restraint—an exasperated Senator Richard Lugar exclaimed, "To imply somehow we need a farm bill in order to feed our troops, to defend our nation, is ridiculous"—the post–September 11 spending spree continued. In the end, lawmakers packed additional billions in spending onto existing agriculture, education, health, and other bills.

As all that was going on, Congress took up debate on an economic stimulus bill. This time, unlike the debates over the anti-terrorism and aviation security bills, lawmakers split along traditional party lines. Republicans used the opportunity to push tax cuts, and Democrats used it to push unemployment and health benefits.

In late October, the House passed, on a mostly party-line 216 to 214 vote, a $100 billion Republican stimulus bill that included a number of the GOP's favorite tax cut proposals from recent years. The bill would have given substantial tax breaks to corporations, including speeding up the write-off on investments and repealing the alternative minimum tax, which would allow some companies to recoup hundreds of millions of dollars in taxes paid since 1986. In addition, the House would have cut capital gains taxes and speeded up the Bush tax cut passed in 2001. Finally, it would give a $300 rebate to Americans who did not qualify for one when the Bush tax cut was originally passed.

The Democratic alternative plan also included the $300 rebate, but almost nothing else from the Republican package. Democrats wanted to spend about $30 billion for unemployment and health care benefits, as well as billions more for new schools and tax benefits—mostly credits—for the poor. Finally, Democrats wanted to cancel a scheduled cut in the income tax rate for the richest Americans.

When the House Republican bill suffered from a torrent of bad press—GOP lawmakers were accused of using the terrorist emergency as an occasion to help their friends in big business—the White House and Senate Republicans intervened to produce a softer version. It increased social spending and toned down tax cuts, but still kept some of the major corporate tax breaks that were in the original proposal. Sensing the upper hand, Senate Majority Leader Tom Daschle rejected the plan, pressing for the inclusion of more unemployment and health care benefits. "We will not even consider a bill unless it has those components," Daschle said on October 30. "To do anything less is a mockery of economic stimulus."

In early November, Senate Democrats pushed their plan through the Finance Committee on a party-line 11 to 10 vote (Vermont's James Jeffords, whose defection six months earlier turned the Senate over to Democratic control, provided the winning vote). But Democrats could not resist throwing a number of special-interest spending provisions into the bill, including money for Amtrak, rural Internet access, and agriculture. That allowed the GOP to portray the Democratic bill as old-fashioned pork-barrel politics. "The stimulus package being considered in the Senate contains $220 million to buy bison meat, cauliflower, eggplant, and pumpkins," White House spokesman Ari Fleischer said. "The president does not understand how that can be stimulative for the economy."

As November dragged on, both sides threw accusations at each other, compromised in tiny steps, and waited to see if events would help them gain the political advantage. But no advantage appeared. By early December, negotiators were still unable to come up with a package that satisfied all sides. On December 9, Vice President Dick Cheney tried to seize the offensive by accusing Daschle of "obstructionist" tactics, which only prompted more counterattacks from Democrats. As Christmas approached, with negotiators still hung up on the issue of health care benefits, both sides began blaming the other for the imminent death of the stimulus package. On December 20, lawmakers officially gave up and went home.

WAR AND ENRON

The moment in which both political parties felt the greatest constraints of bipartisanship turned out to be relatively brief. By late November, two and a half months after the attacks and one month after the passage of the USA Patriot Act, Democrats on Capitol Hill began to openly criticize some of the White

House's anti-terrorism policies in ways that would not have been possible just a few weeks earlier.

At issue was the administration's intention to try some foreign terrorist suspects in military tribunals. Democrats on the Senate Judiciary Committee held a series of hearings to examine the idea, and while they scheduled a number of administration critics to testify, they did not invite anyone from the administration to defend the tribunal policy. Only after a top Justice Department official requested that Criminal Division chief Michael Chertoff be allowed to testify at the first hearing did Democrats give the administration a voice in the proceedings.

When the hearing began, several Democrats were plainly eager to confront Chertoff. "We've stated that military tribunals in Sudan do not provide procedural safeguards," Senator Edward Kennedy began. "We've criticized Burma, China, Colombia, Malaysia, Nigeria, Russia, and Turkey on similar grounds. Yet now we're calling for the use of military tribunals. The concern is, aren't we doing exactly what we've criticized other nations for doing?" Other Democrats followed in a similar vein, and Chertoff was forced to defend administration policies against attacks that were far more pointed and direct than any that occurred during the debate over the USA Patriot Act. Republicans widely believed the hearing, along with a later one at which Attorney General John Ashcroft was summoned to testify, was an indirect way for Democrats to criticize—and score political points against—George W. Bush, whose popularity protected him from direct attack.

Similar scenes unfolded in other committee rooms across Capitol Hill. Indeed, as time passed and the immediate shock of September 11 faded, it gradually became apparent that the president's opponents again had the luxury of opposing the president. As 2002 opened, both sides resumed the battle over tax cuts. They fought over the president's budget proposal (although not over its massive increases in military spending). And they maneuvered furiously to gain political advantage from the collapse of the Enron Corporation.

Indeed, with the war in Afghanistan apparently winding down, the Enron story began to dominate the news in a way that no story had since the terrorist attacks. Almost overnight, multiple and overlapping investigations began in both the House and Senate. Indignant lawmakers dragged former Enron executives before investigating committees to plead the Fifth Amendment while cameras rolled. And Democrats ratcheted up their demands that Vice President Dick Cheney turn over the records of his energy task force, which had met several times with representatives of Enron.

The sudden appearance of Enron was a liberation of sorts for Democratic leaders. The post–September 11 politics of national security had given George W. Bush a huge political advantage and left Democrats in a bind: they did not dare appear unpatriotic by opposing the president, but they also had to find ways to keep themselves in the political ball game. As the initial trauma of the terrorist attacks faded, Democrats looked for openings on issues like military tribunals but achieved only limited success because the public largely supported the Bush administration on nearly every national security issue. Enron, on the other hand, was different; Democrats felt free to demand investigations of the company while stressing its close ties to the Bush administration (and trying to downplay their own Enron connections). That way, they could chip away at Bush without seeming to challenge his role as wartime president.

And chip away they did. On January 24, Daschle accused Bush of "Enronizing" the economy. A few days earlier, Democratic National Committee chairman Terry McAuliffe charged that Bush "seems to be running fiscal policy the way the folks at Enron ran their company." And on February 9, writing in the *New York Times*, Ernest Hollings, the Democratic chairman of the Senate Commerce Committee, called for a special prosecutor to investigate the Bush administration's contacts with Enron. The unfolding scandal, if that is what it was, had developed all the hallmarks of a classic Washington feeding frenzy. There could hardly have been a more vivid sign that the extraordinary period that followed September 11 was over.

DANIEL PIPES

A New Round
of Anger and
Humiliation

Islam After 9/11

"THE WORLD HAS CHANGED," Westerners often say, commenting on the events of September 11, but few Muslims echo that view. In dueling statements issued on October 7, the day the war in Afghanistan began, President George W. Bush and Osama bin Laden exemplified this contrast. While the former referred to the "sudden terror" that had descended on the United States just twenty-seven days earlier, the latter reported that the Muslim world had experienced more than eighty years of "humiliation and disgrace" at American hands, during which its sons were killed and its sanctities defiled. Twenty-seven days versus eighty years sums up the difference between a stunned American sense of ruptured innocence and the brooding militant Islamic feeling of epochal betrayal and trauma. For this and other reasons, the Muslim world was not nearly so jolted by the death of over three thousand Americans as was the West.

More broadly, to understand the impact of September 11 on the Muslim world requires putting aside the response in the West and immersing oneself in Muslim sensibilities. The best place to begin is with an understanding of the deep resentment against the West that bin Laden articulates and so many Muslims share.

ISLAMIC HISTORY AND
HOSTILITY TO THE WEST

This anger has deep roots. From the Islamic religion's origins in the seventh century and for roughly the next millennium, the career of Muslims was one of consistent worldly success. By whatever standard one judged—power, wealth, health, or education—Muslims stood at the pinnacle of global achievement. This connection between accepting the Islamic message and apparent reward by God endured in so many aspects of life in so many places for such a long time that Muslims readily came to assume that mundane well-being was their due as a sign of God's favor. To be Muslim meant to be on the winning team.

But then, starting about 1800, things went awry. Power, wealth, health, and education moved elsewhere, and specifically to Europe, a place long scorned as backward. For two long centuries, Muslims have watched as other peoples, especially Christians, surged ahead. Not only did France, England, and the United States do so on the grandest scale, but more recently East Asia has outpaced the Muslim world. As a result, a sense of failure has suffused Muslim life. If Islam brings God's grace, many Muslims have asked themselves, why then do Muslims fare so poorly? This trauma of things going all wrong is the key to understanding modern Islam.

It has spurred deep questions about what needs to be done

to find the right direction, but few satisfying answers. Despite extensive soul-searching, Muslims have not yet found an answer to the question "What went wrong?" Instead, they have bounced from one scheme to another, finding satisfaction in none of them. A succession of false starts has left Muslims deeply perplexed about their predicament, and not a little frustrated. In all, Muslims sense their own conspicuous lack of success in emerging from the humiliation of their current circumstances.

This sense of failure goes far to explain the acute hostility to the West that prevails in most Muslim societies. Muslims vaguely realize that a thousand years ago, as Martin Kramer puts it, "the Middle East was the crucible of world civilization," whereas today it "sulks on the margins of a world civilization forged in the West."[1] That sulking has translated into anger, envy, hostility, irrational fears, conspiracy theories, and political extremism. These emotions go far to account for the appeal of a host of radical ideologies, both imported (fascism, Leninism) and homegrown (Pan-Arabism, Pan-Syrianism). Each of these movements in turn confirms the sense that the West is the enemy.

These days, the strongest vehicle for such emotions is militant Islam (also known as Islamism), a political movement that takes the religion of Islam and turns it into the basis of a totalitarian ideology that shares much with prior versions, namely fascism and Marxism-Leninism. Like them, for example, it seeks to replace capitalism and liberalism as the reigning world system. The appeal of militant Islam goes far to account for the anti-Western hatred coming from Muslims in many places around the world, including Muslims resident in the West itself.

Islamists discern a long list of countries—Algeria, Turkey,

---

1. Martin Kramer, "Islam's Sober Millennium," December 31, 1999.

Egypt, and Malaysia are prominent examples—where they believe local Muslim rulers are doing the West's dirty business in suppressing their movement. They also have another list—Kashmir, Afghanistan, Chechnya, and Sudan rank high here—where they see the West actively suppressing noble Islamist efforts to establish a just society. Whenever Muslims move toward the emergence of an Islamic state, an Islamist explains, the "treacherous hands of the secular West are always there in the Muslim world to bring about the defeat of the Islamic forces."[2] Islamists see themselves surrounded and besieged by the West. Around the world, they feel, they are stymied by an arrogant and imperialist West.

HATRED OF THE UNITED STATES

In particular, Islamists see the United States as an aggressive force that seeks to steal Muslims' resources, exploit their labor, and undermine their religion. A wide consensus exists that Washington and Hollywood have joined forces to establish a hegemony over the world (the "new world order"). In the words of Ayatollah Khomeini, perhaps the most influential modern interpreter of Islam: "The danger that America poses is so great that if you commit the smallest oversight, you will be destroyed. . . . America plans to destroy us, all of us."[3] In the words of an Egyptian, the Americans "have us by the throat."

This outlook has the crucial implication that violence against Americans is viewed as defensive in nature. That in turn justifies Muslim attempts to harm Americans or even destroy the United States. Ikrama Sabri, Yasir Arafat's man run-

2. Shamim A. Siddiqi, *Methodology of Dawah Ilallah in American Perspective* (Brooklyn, N.Y.: Forum for Islamic Work, 1989), pp. ix–x.
3. Imam Khomeini, *Islam and Revolution*, trans. Hamid Algar (Berkeley, Calif.: Mizan Press, 1981), pp. 286, 306.

ning the Palestinian Authority's religious hierarchy in Jerusalem, often inveighs against the United States in his Friday sermon at Al-Aqsa mosque, a prestigious and influential position. For example, he made this choice plea to God in 1997: "Oh Allah, destroy America, her agents and her allies!"[4]

To dehumanize Americans, fundamentalists portray them in beastlike terms—vermin, dogs, and bacteria—thereby turning them into enemies deserving of extermination. The Westerner, in the view of 'Adil Husayn, a leading Egyptian writer, is "nothing but an animal whose major concern is to fill his belly."[5] Immoral, consumerist, and threatening, he deserves to die. The conspiracy theories that so many Middle Eastern religious establishments espouse also dehumanize Americans, depicting them as cunning plotters grasping at Muslim lands, wealth, and women.

One result is the expression of delight on hearing about American fatalities. Ahmad Jibril, a Palestinian leader, publicly shared his joy on hearing about the loss of life due to the San Francisco earthquake in 1989, then added, "I don't know how I would have managed to take revenge on the United States, but it seems that God did it for me."[6] One also finds such vicious views expressed by Muslims living in the United States itself: Responding to the news of a U.S. Air Force accident not long after, *Islam Report*, a San Diego–based publication, published a headline that read, "O ALLAH, LOCK THEIR THROATS IN THEIR OWN TRAPS!"[7]

This litany of statements points to two facts: Osama bin Laden is not a unique figure but echoes views promoted by

4. Voice of Palestine, on September 12, 1997.
5. *Ash-Sha'b* (Cairo), July 22, 1994.
6. *The Sunday Independent*, November 26, 1989.
7. Quoted in Steven Emerson, "The Other Fundamentalists," *New Republic*, June 12, 1995, p. 30.

some of the most authoritative and influential Islamic authorities; and this viewpoint resonates among Muslims around the world, even including some living in the West.

This context helps explain why the Muslim world responded as it did to the September 11 atrocities, even before it was clear who had perpetrated them. In most of the world, initial reaction to this news was mournful. Peoples and governments alike responded with heartfelt grief and with the sense of common humanity. But among Muslims, the killing of thousands of Americans prompted less a sense of grief than one of pleasure.

"Bull's-eye," commented Egyptian taxi drivers as they watched reruns of the World Trade Center collapse. "It's payback time," said a Cairene. Other Egyptians expressed a wish for George W. Bush to have been buried in the buildings or exulted that this was their most happy moment in decades. And so it went around the Middle East. In Lebanon and the West Bank, Palestinians shot guns into the air, a common way of showing delight. "We're ecstatic," said a Lebanese. In Jordan, Palestinians handed out sweets in another expression of joy.

Outside the Middle East, a good many Muslims expressed the view that Americans got what they deserved. Nigerian papers reported that the Islamic Youth Organization in Zamfara province organized an event to celebrate the attacks. "Whatever destruction America is facing, as a Muslim I am happy," came a typical quote from Afghanistan. A Pakistani leader said that Washington is paying for its policies against Palestinian, Iraqi, Bosnian, and other Muslims, then warned that the "worst is still to come."

Around the Muslim world, nearly identical anti-American slogans were heard over the next weeks: "U.S., Go to Hell!" (Indonesia), "Go To Hell America" (Malaysia), "Death to America" (Bangladesh), "Death to America" (India), "America is the enemy of God" (Oman), "America is a great Satan" (Yemen), "U.S. go to hell" (Egypt), "Down, down USA!" (Sudan).

Most Muslim governments were on best behavior after September 11, decrying the loss of American lives. But here, too, there were cracks. Iranian officialdom, for example, found it very hard to be sympathetic to Americans and insisted on bringing the Arab-Israeli conflict into the discussion. Some analyses connected the terrorism to America's "blind support of the Zionist regime" and others actually accused Israel of organizing the attacks, in a supposed effort to deflect world opinion from its own conflict with the Palestinians. (This subsequently became an accepted verity in many Muslim countries, with elaborate conspiracy theories about the Mossad's role.) In Iraq, not surprisingly, the state-controlled media approved of the violence, commenting that the "the American cowboys are reaping the fruit of their crimes against humanity." It also announced that the "myth of America was destroyed along with the World Trade Center."

LOVE OF BIN LADEN

Even before September 11, Osama bin Laden enjoyed a very high reputation owing to his unremitting hostility to the United States. His biographer, Simon Reeve, wrote in 1999: "Many who had never met him, whose only contact was through one of his interviews, a radio broadcast or Internet homepage, pronounced themselves ready to die for his cause."[8] Hasan at-Turabi, the powerful Sudanese leader, found that bin Laden

8. Simon Reeve, *The New Jackals: Ramzi Yousef, Osama bin Laden, and the Future of Terrorism* (Boston: Northeastern University Press, 1999), p. 203.

had developed "as a champion, as a symbol of Islam for all young people, in the whole Muslim world."[9]

When bin Laden emerged as the man behind the September 11 attacks, his reputation soared to extraordinary heights around the Muslim world. "Long live bin Laden," shouted five thousand demonstrators in the southern Philippines. In Pakistan, bin Laden's face sold merchandise and massive street rallies left two persons dead. Ten thousand marched in the capitals of Bangladesh and Indonesia. In northern Nigeria, bin Laden had (according to Reuters) "achieved iconic status" and his partisans set off religious riots leading to two hundred deaths.[10] Pro–bin Laden demonstrations took place even in Mecca, where overt political activism is unheard of.

Everywhere, the *Washington Post* reported, Muslims cheered on bin Laden "with almost a single voice."[11] The Internet buzzed with odes to him as a man "of solid faith and power of will."[12] A Saudi explained that "Osama is a very, very, very, very good Muslim."[13] A Kenyan added: "Every Muslim is Osama bin Laden."[14] "Osama is not an individual, but a name of a holy war," read a banner in Kashmir.[15] In perhaps the most extravagant statement, one Pakistani declared that "Bin Laden is Islam. He represents Islam."[16] In France, Muslim youths chanted bin Laden's name as they threw rocks at non-Muslims.

Palestinians were especially enamored. According to Hussam Khadir, a member of Arafat's Fatah party, "Bin Laden

9. Quoted in ibid., p. 213.
10. Reuters, October 18 and 14, 2001.
11. *Washington Post*, October 9, 2001.
12. Reuters, October 8, 2001.
13. Time, October 15, 2001.
14. *New York Times*, October 13, 2001.
15. Reuters, October 11, 2001.
16. *New York Times*, September 30, 2001.

today is the most popular figure in the West Bank and Gaza, second only to Arafat."[17] A ten-year-old girl announced that she loves him like a father.[18] Nor was she alone. "Everybody loves Osama bin Laden at this time. He is the most righteous man in the whole world," declared a Palestinian woman.[19] A Palestinian Authority policeman called him "the greatest man in the world . . . our Messiah" even as he (reluctantly) dispersed students who marched in solidarity with the Saudi.[20]

Survey research helps understand these sentiments. In the Palestinian Authority, a Bir Zeit poll found that 26 percent of Palestinians considered the September 11 attacks consistent with Islamic law.[21] In Pakistan, a Gallup poll found a nearly identical 24 percent reaching this conclusion.[22] Even those who consider the attacks on September 11 an act of terrorism (64 percent of both Palestinians and Pakistanis) showed respect for these as acts of political defiance and technical prowess. "Of course we're upset that so many died in New York. But at the same time, we're in awe of what happened," said a young Cairene woman.[23] An online survey of Indonesians found 50 percent seeing bin Laden as a "justice fighter" and 35 percent a terrorist.[24] More broadly, I estimate that bin Laden enjoyed in those first weeks the emotional support of half the Muslim world.

With the exception of one government-staged anti–bin Laden demonstration in Pakistan and very few prominent Is-

---

17. *Boston Globe*, October 10, 2001.
18. *The Independent*, October 11, 2001.
19. *The Guardian*, October 9, 2001.
20. *The Independent*, October 11, 2001.
21. IRI, October 11, 2001.
22. *Newsweek*, October 14, 2001.
23. *Washington Post*, October 9, 2001.
24. Reuters, October 17?, 2001. *http://straitstimes.asia1.com.sg/asia/story/0,1870,77031,00.html*.

lamic scholars, hardly anyone publicly denounced him in September or October 2001. The only Islamic scholar in Egypt who unreservedly condemned the September 11 suicide operations admitted that he is completely isolated.[25] Further, not a single Muslim government came out publicly in support of the American bombings against him. American officials were waiting in vain for Muslim politicians to speak up. "It'd be nice if some leaders came out and said that the idea the U.S. is targeting Islam is absurd," noted one U.S. diplomat.[26] They did not do so because to do so meant to contradict bin Laden's wide adulation.

But then a remarkable change took place.

DISAPPOINTMENT WITH BIN LADEN

The U.S. government began its military campaign in Afghanistan on October 7. For a month, there were no visible results. As late as the morning of November 9, the Taliban regime still ruled the territories that had been under its control for several years—or almost 95 percent of Afghanistan. But then the Taliban rule collapsed. Days later it controlled just 15 percent of the country, and by December 7 it had lost control of Kandahar, its last city, and was on the run in the hills and the caves of Afghanistan, a spent force repudiated widely by joyous Afghans.

This quick change of fortunes resulted in large part from the powerful use of air power by the United States, but also from the lack of perseverance on the part of Taliban troops. Awed by American power, many of them switched sides to the U.S.-backed Northern Alliance. According to one analyst, "De-

25. *Newsweek*, October 15, 2001.
26. *Washington Post*, October 9, 2001.

fections, even in mid-battle, are proving key to the rapid collapse across Afghanistan of the formerly ruling Taliban mili-
tia."[27] American muscle and will made militant Islam a losing
proposition. The force that had ruled their country was disin-
tegrating before their eyes and the Taliban's own forces realized they were on the losing side, having no desire to go down
with it, and decided to do something.

This readiness to switch sides fit into a larger pattern that
became evident within days of November 11; Muslims around
the world sensed the same shift of power away from militant
Islam and they responded similarly.

This was especially evident in Pakistan, where enthusiasm
for the Taliban cause had been extremely high in September
and October 2001. Here is a report, in the *Los Angeles Times*,
starting with an account of the scene in Quetta, near the border
with Afghanistan, on October 8, or one day after hostilities
began: After demonstrators "burned effigies of the American
and Pakistani presidents, set fire to cars, stormed the police
station and smashed shop windows," firebrand religious leaders
addressed 10,000 people in Ayub Stadium each Friday. They
had vengeance in their bellies, they had outrage in their hearts,
their anger came out in such a flood of words that some of them
got hoarse. "The time will come when the American heads are
on one side and our guns are on the other!" one shouted.
"Prepare yourself for jihad, and I assure you that success will
be ours!"

But then, as American military success became clear, the
anti-American zealots lost their nerve. The same stadium that
a month earlier held 10,000 two months later had less than 500
people. "A lone, badly wrinkled poster of Osama bin Laden
bobbed in the front row. After a parade of religious leaders

27. Associated Press, November 17, 2001.

fumed at the microphone about jihad, or holy war, the crowd, which had sat almost silent through two hours of speeches, could barely muster a chorus of *Allahu akbar* (God is great) at the end." In Swat Valley, some 20 percent of the 10 to 15 thousand men who were inspired by cries of *jihad* to go off to fight the United States in Afghanistan did not return. In some cases, the losses were much higher: one Pakistani reported that 41 out of 43 of his comrades lost their lives in Afghanistan.[28] These losses generated intense resentment of the militant Islamic leaders who prodded them to go off to war, unprepared and even unwelcome, while they themselves stayed back in the comfort of their native villages.

Pakistanis turned against the militant Islamic groups, especially those that encouraged devout Muslims to travel to Afghanistan and help the Taliban. For example, Tehrik Nifaz Shariat-e-Mohammedi has acknowledged that two to three thousand of its volunteers are missing and feared dead; the organization's leader, Sufi Muhammad, found himself jailed by the Pakistani authorities when he returned from Afghanistan in November. There is also a widespread anger against him. "We curse Sufi Muhammad for sacrificing so many innocent lives," said one tribal elder. "It is because of him that so many children have become orphans and women widows."[29] More broadly,

> The battle fervor that swept this region at the beginning of the war has largely evaporated, as thousands of foreign volunteer fighters—many of them Pakistani—were left in the gun sights. . . . In these frontier communities, where the mullahs have always had more pull than the government, there is a deepening

---

28. *New York Times*, January 27, 2002.
29. Associated Press, December 11, 2001.

resentment of the religious leaders who called away so many young men to a certain death.[30]

To put it mildly, this is hardly the expected reaction to the American air campaign in Afghanistan, which many analysts predicted would convulse Pakistani society and perhaps even lead to an overthrow of the government by those sympathetic to militant Islam. Instead, a convincing demonstration of U.S. power led to the cowering and retreat of militant Islam.

A similar sequence can be seen in the Arabic-speaking countries. Martin Indyk, the former U.S. ambassador to Israel, noted that in the first week after the U.S. airstrikes began on October 7, nine anti-American demonstrations took place. The second week saw three of them, the third week one, the fourth week, two. "Then—nothing," observes Indyk. "The Arab street is quiet."[31] This is all the more remarkable given that the Arab-Israeli conflict, perhaps the most emotional touchstone of Arab life, heated up considerably at about the same time. A well-traveled reporter came to a similar conclusion:

> nearly two months into an intense military campaign, and half-way through the Muslim holy month of Ramadan, the Arab "street," or public opinion, appears to have responded to bin Laden's call for an anti-Western uprising in the same way it has reacted to similar calls in the past from Islamic militants, Iraqi President Saddam Hussein and others—by changing the channel and proceeding with business.[32]

In fact, the mood rapidly shifted in the opposite direction. For example, in Kuwait, where the law code was close to being brought into line with Islamic requirements and punishments

30. *Los Angeles Times*, December 3, 2001.
31. Newhouse News Service, November 16, 2001.
32. Howard Schneider, "Arab 'Street' Unmoved by News," *Washington Post*, November 30, 2001.

before September 11, the reality of U.S. strength led to a rapid change in mood. "America's swift reaction to the Sept. 11 terror attacks, and the scenes of Afghan joy at abolishing the very same religious restrictions, quickly damped enthusiasm" for such changes, reported the *Wall Street Journal*.[33] "Now, the secular people want to abolish all Islamic rules that are applied in Kuwait or Saudi Arabia. There are even some voices about permitting alcohol."

In similar fashion, the Arab media turned on bin Laden when he began looking like a loser. Generalizing about this trend, the *Washington Post* found that "there has been a clear effort to discredit bin Laden in religious terms and shed light on his criminal bent, political aspirations and pretensions of piety."[34] Indeed, some analysts went so far as to suspect that the damage bin Laden had caused Islam was an Israeli plot! "If world Zionism spent billions of dollars to tarnish the image of Islam, it will not accomplish what the terrorists have done with their actions and words."[35] So far had bin Laden fallen that he was now no better than a tool of the alleged Jewish conspiracy.

The same patterns can be found throughout the Muslim world, in such countries as Indonesia, India, and Nigeria, where the overwrought passions of September quickly became distant memories.

American military success so encouraged the authorities that they began, finally, to crack down. This was again most evident in Pakistan. "There has been a profound shift in the politics of religious extremism in Pakistan over the last few weeks," reported the *Los Angeles Times* on December 10, 2001, which went on to explain that the government for years had

33. December 31, 2001.
34. *Washington Post*, November 23, 2001.
35. Nabil Luka Bibawi in *Al-Ahram*, cited in ibid.

permitted militant Islamic groups to operate with almost total freedom, but seeing which way the wind was now blowing, it began to "rein in the jihad organizations and check their pervasive influence on the nation's educational, political and social welfare systems." Those Swat Valley preachers, for example, found themselves behind bars. The most significant step came on January 12, 2002, when President Pervez Musharraf attacked militant Islam in a major speech ("The day of reckoning has come. Do we want Pakistan to become a theocratic state?") that one observer suggested "has the potential—the potential—to be the kind of mind-set–shattering breakthrough for the Muslim world that has not been seen since Anwar el-Sadat's 1977 visit to Israel."[36] Making good on his word, in just the first week after this historic speech, Musharraf had government forces close hundreds of religious offices and arrest over two thousand people. Militant Islamic groups aired much displeasure with these steps but did almost nothing to obstruct them ("We cannot fight against our own state, we can only wait for a better time").[37]

This pattern was replicated in other countries. The effective ruler of Saudi Arabia admonished religious leaders to be careful and responsible in their statements ("weigh each word before saying it")[38] after he saw that Washington meant business. Likewise, the Egyptian government moved more aggressively against its militant Islamic elements. In Yemen, the government cracked down on the Islamist foreigners coming into the country. Similarly, in China, the government prohibited the selling of badges celebrating Osama bin Laden ("I am bin

36. Thomas L. Friedman, "Pakistan's Constitution Avenue," *New York Times*, January 20, 2002.
37. Reuters, January 18, 2002.
38. *Arab News*, November 15, 2001.

Laden. Who should I fear?")[39] only *after* the U.S. victories began. Ironically, the same strengthening of resolve could be seen in the United States itself; after monitoring the Holy Land Foundation, an Islamic "charitable" foundation, since 1993, the federal government finally closed it down in December 2001 when it felt the confidence that came from its own successful military campaign.

9/11 VS. 11/9

The events of the brief three-month period following September 11 send a powerful and unambiguous message about the fortunes of militant Islam and the exercise of power.

If militant Islam achieved the acme of its achievement on 9/11, then 11/9 could be when the movement began its descent. The first date marked the peak of militant Islam, its day of greatest success in humiliating the West, causing death and panic. The second date, when the Taliban lost their first major city, marked an apparent turning point, with the West finding its resolve and its strength to deal with its new main enemy.

The marked contrast between these two dates has several implications for understanding the Muslim world. First, public opinion in the Muslim world is volatile, responding to developing events in an emotional, superficial, and changeable way. Second, as the *Los Angeles Times* notes, "popular support for militant Islam is not nearly so broad as was once believed."[40] The movement is loud and it is vociferous, but it does not command more than a small minority of the Muslim world's active support. Third, that militant Islam is a bit of a paper tiger—ferocious when unopposed but quite easily intimidated.

---

39. Associated Press, November 17, 2001, quoting *Beijing Youth Daily*.
40. *Los Angeles Times*, December 3 and 10, 2001.

Fourth, the so-called "street" has little bearing on developments. It rises up with much noise but without much consequence, unable to force governments to take its preferred actions. It dies down when its favorite causes fare poorly.

This is not to deny that much anger continues to be directed against the United States ("Jihad will continue until doomsday, or until America is defeated, either way")[41] or that in some circles bin Laden retains his appeal (one Afghan: "to me, he is a god").[42] It is only to say that American strength and resolve make these sentiments less likely to become operational.

U.S. POLICY IMPLICATIONS

For two decades—from the time Ayatollah Khomeini reached power in Iran in 1979 with "Death to America" as his slogan—U.S. embassies, planes, ships, and barracks were assaulted, leading to hundreds of American deaths. These attacks took place around the world, especially in the Middle East and Europe, but also in the United States itself. In the face of this persistent assault, Washington barely responded. The policy through those years was to view the attacks as no more than a sequence of discrete criminal incidents, and not as part of a sustained military assault on the country. This approach had several consequences. It meant:

- Focusing on the arrest and trial of the dispensable characters who actually carried out violent acts, leaving the funders, planners, organizers, and commanders of terrorism to continue their work unscathed, prepared to carry out more attacks.

41. *New York Times*, January 27, 2002.
42. *The Times* (London), January 19, 2002.

- Relying primarily on such defensive measures as metal detectors, security guards, bunkers, police arrests, and prosecutorial eloquence—rather than on such offensive tools as soldiers, aircraft, and ships.

- Seeing the terrorists' motivations as criminal, ignoring the extremist ideologues involved.

- Ignoring the fact that terrorist groups (and the states that support them) have declared war on the United States (sometimes publicly).

- Requiring that the U.S. government have levels of proof that can stand up in a U.S. court of justice before deploying military force, assuring that in the vast majority of cases there would be a subdued response to the killing of Americans.

As Muslims watched militant Islam hammer away at Americans and American interests, they could not but conclude that the United States, for all its resources, was tired and soft. Not knowing the nature of democracy—slow to be aroused but relentless when angered—they marveled at the audacity of militant Islam and its ability to get away with its attacks. This awe culminated in the aftermath of September 11, when Osama bin Laden and the Taliban leader called openly for nothing less than the "extinction of America."[43] At that time, this did not seem beyond reach.

These ambitious claims shed light on the goals of the September 11 attacks. Although one cannot be sure of their purpose, it makes sense that they were intended severely to weaken the United States. Judging from militant Islam's previous successes, al-Qaeda must have thought that it would get

43. Associated Press, November 15, 2001.

away with this attack with no more than the usual criminal probe. Further, having seen both the American unwillingness to absorb casualties and the damage the Afghanistan-based Islamists did to the Soviet Union a decade and more earlier, al-Qaeda probably thought that its hits would demoralize the American population and lead to civil unrest, perhaps even beginning a sequence of events that would eventually lead to the U.S. government's collapse. If this was their thinking, they probably counted on the American police protecting government buildings, not tracking down al-Qaeda operatives.

How could bin Laden and his colleagues know that their acts would lead to a rousing call to arms? Why should 240 deaths in a Beirut barracks lead to no retaliation and just over three thousand deaths on the East Coast mobilize the country in a way not seen since Pearl Harbor? One can hardly fault them for not having foreseen this shift. It has something to do with the mysterious forces of democracy and public opinion, about which they are highly ignorant.

Even less could they have understood that a paradigm shift took place on September 11, whereby terrorism left the domain of criminality and entered that of warfare. This change had many implications. It meant no longer targeting just the foot soldiers who actually carry out the violence but the organizations and governments standing behind them. It meant relying on the armed forces, not policemen. It meant defense overseas rather than in American courtrooms. It meant dispensing with the unrealistically high expectations of proof so that when reasonable evidence points to a regime or organization having harmed Americans, U.S. military force can be deployed. It meant using force so that the punishment is disproportionately greater than the attack. It also meant that, as in conventional war, America's military need not know the names and specific actions of enemy soldiers before fighting them. There is no need to know the precise identity of a perpetrator; in war, there are times when one strikes first and asks questions later.

It might seem mysterious that the military model was not adopted earlier, it being so obviously more appropriate than the criminal one. But the fact is, it is also much more demanding of Americans, requiring a readiness to spend money and lose lives over a long period. Force works only if it is part of sustained policy, not a one-time event. Throwing a few bombs (such as was done against the Libyan regime in 1986 and against sites in Afghanistan and Sudan in 1998) does not amount to a serious policy. Going the military route requires a long-term commitment that demands much from Americans over many years.

The pattern is clear: So long as Americans submitted passively to murderous attacks by militant Islam, this movement gained support among Muslims. When Americans finally took up arms to fight militant Islam, its forces were overwhelmed and its appeal quickly diminished. Victory on the battlefield, in other words, has not only the obvious advantage of protecting the United States but also the important side-effect of lancing the anti-American boil that spawned those attacks in the first place.

The implication is clear: There is no substitute for victory. If the U.S. government wishes to weaken its strategic enemy, militant Islam, it must take two steps. First, continue the war on terror globally, using appropriate means, starting with Afghanistan but going on to wherever militant Islam poses a threat, in Muslim-majority countries (such as Saudi Arabia), in Muslim-minority countries (such as the Philippines), and even in the United States itself. As this effort brings success, secondly Washington should promote moderate Muslims. Not only will they represent a wholesome change from the totalitarianism of militant Islam but they, and they alone, can address the trauma of Islam and propose ideas that will ease the way for one sixth of humanity fully to modernize.

Ironically, while Muslims did not feel the impact of September 11 as intensely as did Westerners, it is they in the long run who might well be far more profoundly affected by it.

ROGER KIMBALL

What We Are
Fighting For

The Example
of Pericles

MIDWAY THROUGH the long article on Afghanistan in the great eleventh edition of the *Encyclopedia Britannica*, one comes across this description of the inhabitants of that ancient mountain country:

> The Afghans, inured to bloodshed from childhood, are familiar with death, and audacious in attack, but easily discouraged by failure; excessively turbulent and unsubmissive to law or discipline; apparently frank and affable in manner, especially when they hope to gain some object, but capable of the grossest brutality when that hope ceases. They are unscrupulous in perjury, treacherous, vain and insatiable, passionate in vindictiveness, which they will satisfy at the cost of their own lives and in the most cruel manner. Nowhere is crime committed on such trifling grounds, or with such general impunity, though when it is punished the punishment is atrocious. Among themselves the Afghans are quarrelsome, intriguing and distrustful; estrangements and affrays are of constant occurrence; . . . The Afghan

is by breed and nature a bird of prey. If from habit and tradition
he respects a stranger within his threshold, he yet considers it
legitimate to warn a neighbour of the prey that is afoot, or even
overtake and plunder his guest after he has quitted his roof.

That refreshingly frank passage, by Colonel Sir Thomas Hungerford Holdich, was published in 1910. I hope that the American and British troops now enjoying the hospitality of the
Afghans are acquainted with this travel advisory. It is as perti-
nent today—in early 2002—as it was one hundred years ago.

I was put in mind of Sir Thomas's insightful commentary
just before Christmas, 2001, when the *New York Times* took its
quote of the day from one Faqir Muhammad, an officer in one
of the many squabbling anti-Taliban armies: "This is what
Afghanistan is," he said. "We kill each other."

Indeed. And not only each other, of course.

Sir Thomas's remarks are valuable not only because of their
contemporaneity but also because they help us set today's issues in historical context. "The farther backward you can look,"
Winston Churchill once observed, "the farther forward you are
likely to see." Early in the Peloponnesian War, a plague swept
through Athens, killing thousands and demoralizing the survivors. In a rallying speech, Pericles (himself soon to die) noted
that "When things happen suddenly, unexpectedly, and against
all calculation, it takes the heart out of a man." Against the
temptations of apathy and acquiescence, Pericles urged his
listeners to recall the greatness of Athens, to face calamity with
an "unclouded mind and react quickly against it."

As the shock of September 11 gives way to the reality of
America at war, it is useful to take a page from Churchill and
cast a backward glance. The pressure of contemporary events
crowds us into the impatient confines of the present, rendering
us insensible to the lessons of history—not least the lesson that

tomorrow's dramas are typically unforeseen by the scripts we abide by today. Language itself conspires to keep us in the dark. I will return in a moment to Pericles. But I want first to dwell briefly on our tendency to use language to emasculate surprise. What a large quota of optimism language budgets into our lives! Already the consolations of normalcy have returned to everyday life. The fresh horror of the attacks has been domesticated—by time, by retribution, by the seemingly endless flow of words that have embroidered the event, analyzing, ordering, explaining. Out of the reestablishment of order, out of explanation, comes hope. And it is worth noting how regularly, in ways small and large, hopefulness insinuates itself into our plans and projects.

Consider only that marvelous phrase "the foreseeable future." With what cheery abandon we employ it! Yet what a nugget of unfounded optimism those three words encompass. How much of the future, really, do we foresee? A week? A day? A minute? "In a minute," as T. S. Eliot said in "The Love Song of J. Alfred Prufrock," "there is time / For decisions and revisions which a minute will reverse." So much of life is a juggling with probabilities, a conjuring with uncertainties, that we often forget upon what stupendous acts of faith even the prudent conduct of life depends.

Had I been asked, on September 10, 2001, whether New York's Twin Towers would continue standing for "the foreseeable future," I should have answered "Yes." And so, in one sense, they did. Only my foresight was not penetrating enough, not far-seeing enough, to accommodate that most pedestrian of eventualities: an event.

An event is as common as dirt. It is also as novel as tomorrow's dawn. "There is nothing," the French writer Charles Péguy noted in the early years of the twentieth century, "so unforeseen as an event."[1] The particular event Péguy had in mind was the Dreyfus Affair. Who could have predicted that the fate of an obscure Jewish army captain falsely accused of spying would have such momentous consequences? And yet this unforeseen event, as Proust observed in his great novel, suddenly, catastrophically, "divided France from top to bottom."[2] Its repercussions were felt for decades. We plan, stockpile, second-guess, buy insurance, make allowances, assess risks, play the odds, envision contingencies, calculate interest, tabulate returns, save for a rainy day . . . and still we are constantly surprised.

In a thoughtful essay called "What Is Freedom?" the philosopher Hannah Arendt noted the extent to which habit—what she disparages somewhat with the name "automatism"—rules life. We are creatures of habit, schedules, and conventions. And thank God for that. For without habit we could never build character. And yet we are also creatures who continually depart from the script. Human beings do not simply *behave* in response to stimuli. We *act*—which means that our lives, though orchestrated largely by routine, are at the same time everywhere edged with the prospect of novelty. "Every act," Arendt wrote,

> seen from the perspective not of the agent but of the process in whose framework it occurs and whose automatism it interrupts, is a "miracle"—that is, something which could not be expected.
> . . . It is in the very nature of every new beginning that it breaks

1. Charles Péguy, "Memories of Youth" in *Temporal and Eternal*, translated by Alexander Dru (Liberty Fund, 2001), p. 70.
2. Marcel Proust, *Remembrance of Things Past*, vol. 2, translated by C. K. Moncrieff and Terence Kilmartin (Random House, 1981), p. 307. Proust, incidentally, shared Péguy's awe in the face of the unexpected: "[W]henever society is momentarily stationary," Proust wrote earlier in *Remembrance of Things Past*, "the people who live in it imagine that no further change will occur, just as, in spite of having witnessed the birth of the telephone, they decline to believe in the aeroplane," vol. 1, p. 557.

into the world as an "infinite improbability," and yet it is precisely this infinitely improbable which actually constitutes the
very texture of everything we call real.[3]

   Every moment of every day presents us with the potential
for what Arendt calls the "miracle" of human action, so familiar
and yet ultimately unfathomable. That is why we find proleptic
phrases like "the foreseeable future" indispensable. They declare the flag of our confidence, the reach of our competence.
They domesticate the intractable mystery of everyday novelty.
But they also serve to remind us that our confidence is deeply
complicit with luck—that most fickle of talismans—our competence instantly revocable without notice. Which is to say that
our foresight is always an adventure, practiced at the pleasure
of the unpredictable.

   This is something that P. G. Wodehouse, a philosopher of
a somewhat merrier stamp than Hannah Arendt, put with his
customary grace when his character Psmith observed that "in
this life . . . we must always distinguish between the Unlikely
and the Impossible."[4] On September 10 it was unlikely that a
small band of murderous fanatics should destroy the Twin
Towers and fundamentally alter the political landscape of the
world. It was not, alas, impossible.

   The eruption of the unlikely is an affront to our complacency, an insult to our pride. We tend to react by subsequently
endowing the unlikely with a pedigree of explanation. This
reassures us by neutralizing novelty, extracting the element of
the unexpected from what actually happened. I think again of
Churchill. Summarizing the qualities that a budding politician
should possess, he adduced both "The ability to foretell what

   3. Hannah Arendt, "What is Freedom?" in *Between Past and Future: Eight
Exercises in Political Thought* (Penguin Books, 1978), p. 169.
   4. P. G. Wodehouse, *Leave it to Psmith* (Vintage, 1975), p. 128.

is going to happen tomorrow, next week, next month, next year"—and the compensating ability "afterwards to explain why it didn't happen."[5]

Today, the events of September 11 can seem almost inevitable. Reasons have been furnished for every detail. Pundits have rehearsed knowing genealogies for all the actors. Plausible itineraries have been repeated until they seem like predictions. All of those reasons and explanations were available on September 10. A look at the literature shows that some had been propounded for years. But they lacked the traction that events give to hindsight. Where were they when they were needed, at 8:00 A.M. on September 11? They were not part of the foreseeable future until that future, unforeseen, overtook us.

I mention these homely incapacities to provide a kind of signpost or reminder. Even the extraordinary circumstance of wartime begets its anesthetizing versions of the ordinary. Our complacency exposed us to surprise on September 11. New complacencies now compete for our allegiance. In part, this results from the pressure of familiarity. Sooner or later, a state of permanent emergency comes to seem like a normal state of affairs. Ceaseless vigilance by nature ceases to be vigilant. But there are other ingredients involved in the return of complacency. Already one senses impatience on the part of the media. From the very beginning of this conflict, President Bush warned that the struggle against terrorism was going to be long, that it would be measured in years, not weeks or months. But a protracted battle does not accord well with a 24-hour news cycle, with the demand for screaming headlines, new developments, clear victories.

5. Winston Churchill, *The Churchill Wit*, edited by Bill Adler (Coward-McCann, 1965), p. 4.

There is no single antidote to these liabilities. Nevertheless, Churchill was right about history providing the best corrective to our myopia. We need to look backwards if we are to extricate ourselves from the constrictions of the present. The "relevance" sought for the present time is best acquired from guideposts that have outlived the hectoring gabble of contemporary fashion. We are often asked if our "values" have kept pace, have "evolved," with the dramatic changes our political and social reality has seen in the past several decades. But values, I think, do not so much "evolve" as change keys. That is to say, our underlying humanity—with its essential moral needs and aspirations—remains constant. And this is why, for example, the emotional and psychological taxonomy that Aristotle provides in his *Ethics* and *Rhetoric* is as fresh and relevant to humanity today as it was two and a half millennia ago.

MODELS OF FREEDOM

Which brings me back to Pericles. What lessons does the great Greek statesman have for us today? Does his example as a leader of the Athenians at the beginning of the Peloponnesian War have a special pertinence for us as we embark on what promises to be a long struggle with an often faceless foe? Does Pericles, in short, point the way for us?

To answer these questions, one first wants to know: what is it that Pericles stood for? To what sort of society was he pointing? What way of life, what vision of the human good did he propound?

In his history of the Peloponnesian War, Thucydides recounts the public funeral oration that Pericles, as commander of the army and first citizen of Athens, delivered to commemorate those fallen after the first year—the first of twenty-seven,

be it noted—of war with Sparta.[6] The short speech is deserv-
edly one of the most famous in history.

The funeral oration outlines the advantages of Athenian
democracy, a bold new system of government that was not
simply a political arrangement but a way of life. There were
two keynotes to that way of life: freedom and tolerance, on the
one hand, responsible behavior and attention to duty on the
other.

The two go together. We Athenians, Pericles said, are "free
and tolerant in our private lives; but in public affairs we keep
to the law"—including, he added in an important proviso,
"those unwritten laws"—the lawlike commands of taste, man-
ners, and morals—"which it is an acknowledged shame to
break." Freedom and tolerance, Pericles suggested, were blos-
soms supported by roots that reached deep into the soil of duty.

Athens had become the envy of the world, partly because
of its wealth, partly because of its splendor, partly because of
the freedom enjoyed by its citizens. Athens' navy was unri-
valed, its empire unparalleled, its civic and cultural institutions
unequalled. The city was "open to the world," a cosmopolitan
center, political life was "free and open," as was private life:
"We do not get into a state with our next-door neighbor,"
Pericles said, "if he enjoys himself in his own way."

Of course, from the perspective of twenty-first century
America, democracy in Athens may seem limited and imper-
fect. Women were entirely excluded from citizenship in Athens
and there was a large slave class that underwrote the material
freedom of Athens' citizens. These things must be acknowledged. But must they be apologized for? Whenever fifth-century Athens is mentioned these days, it seems that what is

6. The funeral oration runs from book 2.35 to 2.65 of Thucydides'
History. I follow the Rex Warner translation.

stressed is not the achievement of Athenian democracy but its limitations.

To my mind, concentrating on the limitations of Athenian democracy would be like complaining that the Wright brothers neglected to provide transatlantic service with their airplanes. The extraordinary achievement of Athens was to formulate the ideal of equality before the law. To be sure, that ideal was not perfectly instantiated in Athens. Perhaps it never will be perfectly instantiated, it being in the nature of ideals to inspire emulation but also to exceed it.

The point to bear in mind is that both the ideal of equality before the law and the cultivation of an open, tolerant society were new. They made Athens the model of democracy for all the republics that sought to follow the path of freedom—just as America is the model of freedom today. Pericles was right to boast that "Future ages will wonder at us, as the present age wonders at us now." To continue the theme of aviation, we might say that in Athens, after innumerable trials elsewhere, democracy finally managed to get off the ground and stay aloft. In Periclean Athens what mattered in assuming public responsibility, as Pericles said, was "not membership in a particular class, but the actual ability which the man possesses." To an extraordinary extent, within the limits of its franchise, Athens lived up to that ideal.

It is also worth noting that life in Athens was not only free but also full. When the day's work was done, Pericles boasted, Athenians turned not simply to private pleasure but also to ennobling recreation "of all kinds for our spirits." For the Age of Pericles was also the age of the great dramatists, the age of Socrates, the great artist Phidias, and others. Freedom, skill, and ambition conspired to make Athens a cultural as well as a political paragon.

A recurrent theme of the funeral oration is the importance

of sound judgment, what Aristotle codified as the virtue of prudence. The blessing of freedom requires the ballast of duty, and informed judgment is the indispensable handmaiden of duty. A free society is one that nurtures the existential slack that tolerance and openness generate. Chaos and anarchy are forestalled by the intervention of politics in the highest sense of the term: deliberation and decision about securing the good life. When it comes to cultural activities, Pericles said, Athenians had learned to love beauty with moderation—the Greek word is *euteleias*, "without extravagance"—and to pursue philosophy and the life of the mind "without effeminacy," *aneu malakias*.[7] Culture and the life of the mind were to be ennoblements of life, not an escape from its burdens, not a decadent pastime.

The exercise of sound judgment was required in other spheres as well. In their conduct of policy, Athenians strove to be bold, but prudent, that is, effective. "We are," Pericles wrote, "capable at the same time of taking risks and of estimating them beforehand." The exercise of sound judgment was not simply an intellectual accomplishment; it was the tithe

---

7. In "The Crisis in Culture," Hannah Arendt provocatively suggests that Pericles "is saying something like this: 'We love beauty within the limits of political judgment, and we philosophize without the barbarian vice of effeminacy.'" Arendt links political judgment with "that curious and ill-defined capacity we commonly call taste": "The activity of taste decides how this world, independent of its utility and our vital interests in it, is to look and sound . . . [I]ts interest in the world is purely 'disinterested,' and that means that neither the life interests of the individual nor the moral interests of the self are involved." Like political judgments, she says, judgments of taste operate by persuasion rather than demonstration, "the judging person—as Kant says quite beautifully—can only 'woo the consent of everyone else' in the hope of coming to an agreement with him eventually, This 'wooing' or persuading corresponds closely to what the Greeks called *peithein*, the convincing and persuading speech which they regarded as the typically political form of people talking with one another." See *Between Past and Future*, pp. 213–24.

of citizenship. "We do not say that a man who takes no interest in politics is a man who minds his own business," Pericles observed, "we say that he has no business here at all." He did not mean that every citizen had to be a politician. What he meant was that all citizens had a common stake in the commonwealth of the city. And that common stake brought with it common responsibilities as well as common privileges. At a time when everyone is clamoring for his or her "rights"—when new "rights" pop up like mushrooms throughout society—it is worth remembering that every right carries with it a corresponding duty. We enjoy certain rights because we discharge corresponding responsibilities. Some rights may be inalienable; none is without price.

Something similar can be said about democracy. Today, the word "democracy" and its cognates are often used as fancy synonyms for mediocrity. When we read about plans to "democratize" education or the arts or athletics, we know that is shorthand for plans to eviscerate those activities, for lowering standards and pursuing them as instruments of racial or sexual redress or some other form of social engineering. Tocqueville was right to warn about the dangers of generalizing the principle of equality that underlies democracy. Universalized, the principle of equality leads to egalitarianism, the ideology of equality.

The problem today is that the egalitarian imperative threatens to overwhelm that other great social impulse, the impulse to achieve, to excel, to surpass: "always to be best and to rise above others," as Homer put it in one classic expression of the agonistic spirit. Radical egalitarianism—egalitarianism uncorrected by the aspirations of excellence—would have us pretend that there are no important distinctions among people; where the pretense is impossible, it would have us enact compensatory programs to minimize, or at least to paper over, the differences.

The results are a vast increase in self-deception, cultural degradation, and bureaucratic meddlesomeness.

It is refreshing to turn to Pericles and remind ourselves that a passion for democracy need not entail the pursuit of mediocrity. Democracy is a high-maintenance form of government. Freedom requires the disciplines of restraint and circumspection if it is to flourish. Athenian democracy was animated by freedom, above all the freedom to excel, and it inspired in citizens both a healthy competitive spirit and "shame," as Pericles said, at the prospect of "falling below a certain standard."

In all this, Pericles noted, Athens was "an education to Greece," a model for its neighbors. At the moment he spoke, at the beginning of a long and ultimately disastrous war, his words must have had special resonance. In celebrating what the Athenians had achieved, he was also reminding them of all they stood to lose. His funeral oration was therefore not only an elegy but also a plea for resoluteness and a call to arms. It is a call that resonates with special significance now that the United States and indeed all of what used to be called Christendom is under attack by a worldwide network of terrorists. Pericles was right: The open society depends upon the interdiction of forces calculated to destroy. "We who remain behind," he said, "may hope to be spared the fate [of the fallen], but must resolve to keep the same daring spirit against the foe."

The view of society and the individual's responsibility that Pericles put forward was rooted in tradition but oriented toward the future. He did not think much of the custom of public funeral orations, he said, but he felt bound to observe it: "This institution was set up and approved by our forefathers, and it is my duty to follow the tradition." At the same time Pericles reminds us of the claims of the future by stressing the future's main emissaries: the children of Athens. "It is impossible," he suggests, "for a man to put forward fair and honest views about our affairs if he has not . . . children whose lives may be at stake."

The vision of society that Pericles articulated in the funeral oration has exercised a permanent fascination on the political imagination of the West. Although occasionally lost sight of, it has always returned to inspire apostles of freedom and tolerance. But it is imperative that we understand that the view of society that Pericles described is not inevitable. It represents a *choice*—a choice, moreover, that must constantly be renewed. It is one version of the good life for man. There are other, competing versions that we would find distinctly less attractive. In the West, Pericles' vision, modified by time and circumstance, has proved to be a peculiarly powerful one. It was absorbed by Christendom in the eighteenth century and helped to inform the democratic principles that undergird British and American democracy.

But we would be untrue to Pericles' counsel of vigilance were we to think that some of the alternatives to this vision were incapable of inspiring strong allegiance. This was true when Pericles spoke. His entire speech presupposes the contrast between the Athenian way of life and another that was inimical to it. It continues to be true. The spectacle of radical Islamists dancing joyfully in the street when news broke of the September 11 attacks on New York and Washington should remind us of that fact.

Indeed, the status of Pericles' vision of society as one alternative among others was dramatically sharpened by the events of September 11. For that attack was not simply an attack on symbols of American capitalism or American military might. Nor was it simply a terrorist attack on American citizens. It was all those things but more. It was an attack on the idea of America as a liberal democratic society, which means that it was an attack on an idea of society that had one of its primary sources in the ideals enunciated by Pericles. It was, as Binyamin Netanyahu put it, a furious salvo in "a war to reverse the triumph of the West." Netanyahu's words should be constantly borne in mind lest the emollient tide of rationalization blunt the angry reality of those attacks.

SHATTERED ILLUSIONS

Many illusions were challenged on September 11. One illusion concerns the fantasies of academic multiculturalists, so-called. I say "so-called" because what goes under the name of multi-culturalism in our colleges and universities today is really a polysyllabic form of mono-culturalism fueled by ideological hatred. Genuine multiculturalism involves a great deal of work, beginning with the arduous task of learning other languages, something most of those who call themselves multiculturalists are conspicuously loath to do.

Think of the fatuous attack on "dead white European males" that stands at the center of the academic multiculturalist enterprise. As a specimen of that maligned species, one could hardly do better than Pericles. Not only is he a dead white European male, but he is one who embodied in his life and aspirations an ideal of humanity completely at odds with aca-demic multiculturalism. He was patriarchal, militarist, elitist, and Eurocentric, indeed, Hellenocentric, which is even worse.

The good news is that Pericles survived September 11. The spurious brand of multiculturalism that encourages us to re-pudiate "dead white European males" and insists that all cul-tures are of equal worth may finally be entering a terminal stage. Figures like Edward Said and Susan Sontag, Harold Pinter, and Noam Chomsky continue to bay about the iniquity of America, the depredations of capitalism, and so on, but their voices have been falling on increasingly deaf ears. The liberal media began by wringing its hands and wondering whether the coalition would hold, whether we were fair to "moderate" members of the Taliban, whether the Afghans were too wily for Americans, whether the United States was acting in too "unilateral" a fashion. On Christmas Eve, in a masterpiece of understatement, the *Wall Street Journal* ran a story under the headline "In War's Early Phase, News Media Showed a Tendency to Misfire." "This war is in trouble," quoth Daniel Schorr on NPR. At the end of October, R. W. Apple warned readers of the *New York Times* that "signs of progress are sparse." Et cetera. Every piece of possible bad news was—and is—touted as evidence that we may have entered a "quagmire," that we are "overextended," "arrogant," "unresponsive" to the needs and desires of indigenes. It is too soon to say which way the rhetorical chips will ultimately fall. But, as of this writing anyway, a constant string of victories has the liberal pundits frustrated and baffled. They had been waiting for a repeat of Vietnam, and the Bush administration disobliged by giving them a conflict in which America was in the right and was winning.

The hollowness of the left-liberal wisdom about the war brings me to another illusion that was challenged by the events of 9/11. I mean the illusion that the world is basically a benevolent, freedom-loving place, and that if only other people had enough education, safe sex, and access to National Public Radio they would become pacific celebrants of democracy and tolerance. This is the temptation of utopia—Greek for "nowhere"—and it must be acknowledged that America's fortunate geographical position in the world has long encouraged certain versions of this temptation. The extraordinary growth of America's wealth and military power in the twentieth-century—like Athens' great wealth and power in the fifth-century B.C.—have kept the wolf from the door and the marauder from our throats. They have also abetted the illusion of invulnerability. But in-

creased international mobility and the widespread dissemina-
tion of technological know-how have conspired to neutralize or
at least attenuate those advantages. September 11, which
brought the destruction of foreign attack to American soil for
the first time since the War of 1812, made it abundantly clear
that we have implacable enemies, enemies we cannot hide
from, effectively appease, or negotiate with, enemies that will
struggle to the death to destroy us. "Allah Akbar!" shout a group
of Taliban prisoners, and then they set about detonating hand
grenades, killing themselves and their guards. The supreme
Taliban leader Mullah Mohammed Omar put it with all possible clarity when he said that for him and his followers "The
real matter is the extinction of America, and God willing, it will
fall to the ground."

A third illusion that was challenged on September 11 concerns the morality of power. It has been fashionable among
trendy academics, CNN commentators, and other armchair
utopians to pretend that the use of power by the powerful is by
definition evil. Violence on the part of anyone claiming to be a
victim was excused as the product of "frustration" or "rage"—
emotions that for mysterious reasons are held to be exonerating
for the dispossessed but incriminating when exhibited by legitimate authority. Hence the ponderous scramble to uncover
"root causes": that is, the search for sociological alibis that might
absolve the perpetrators of evil from the inconveniences of
guilt. Another quotation from Charles Péguy: "Surrender is
essentially an operation by means of which we set about explaining instead of acting."

This favorite liberal pastime has not been abandoned, but
it looks increasingly rancid. As the commentator Jonathan
Rauch wittily put it shortly after the terrorist attacks, the cause
of terrorism is terrorists. September 11 reminded us that with
power comes responsibility. Power without resolution is per-

ceived as weakness, and weakness is always dangerously provocative. In the aftermath of September 11, we in the West
have often been cautioned against exciting Islamic rage. My
own feeling is that it is salutary for our allies and our enemies
alike to understand that American rage, too, is an unpleasant
thing. Pericles commended the Athenians on their "adventur-
ous" spirit that had "forced an entry into every sea and into
every land." Everywhere, he noted, Athens "left behind . . .
everlasting memorials of good done to our friends or suffering
inflicted on our enemies."

Since the 1970s, we have tended to flinch from such frank
talk; we shy away from talk of forcing anyone to do anything;
we seem ashamed of acknowledging that we have enemies let
alone acknowledging that we wish them ill; we are embarrassed
alike by the perquisites and the obligations of power. Such
squeamishness is precisely part of the "effeminacy" against
which Pericles warned. We desperately wish to be liked. We
forget that true affection depends upon respect.

At least since the end of the Vietnam conflict, the United
States has vacillated in discharging its responsibilities to power.
Whatever the wisdom of our involvement in Vietnam, our way
of extricating ourselves was ignominious and an incitement to
further violence. The image of that U.S. helicopter evacuating
people from our embassy in Saigon is a badge of failure, not so
much of military strategy but of nerve.

Even worse was our response to the hostage crisis in Iran
in 1979 and 1980. Our hesitation to act decisively was duly
noted and found contemptible by our enemies. And the fiasco
of President Carter's botched rescue attempt, when a transport
vehicle and one of our helicopters collided on the sands of the
Iranian desert, was a national humiliation. President Reagan
did effectively face down the Soviet Union, but his halfhearted

response to the terrorist bombing of a U.S. Marine barracks in Lebanon in 1983 contributed to the tattered reputation of America as (in Mao's phrase) "a paper tiger."

The Clinton administration sharply exacerbated the problem. From 1993 through 2000, United States again and again demonstrated its lack of resolve even as it let the U.S. military infrastructure decay. In Somalia at the end of 1992, two U.S. helicopters were shot down, several Americans were killed, the body of one was dragged naked through the streets of Mogadishu. We did nothing—an action, or lack of action, that prompted Osama bin Laden way back then to reflect that his followers were "surprised at the low morale of the American soldiers and realized more than before that the American soldier was a paper tiger and after a few blows ran in defeat."

It was the same in 1993, when terrorists bombed the World Trade Center, killing six people and wounding scores. Bin Laden applauded the action but denied responsibility. No one really believed him; nevertheless nothing was done. (One of the wretches jailed for that atrocity commented: "Next time we'll do it right.")

It was the same in June 1996, when a truck bomb exploded outside a U.S. military barracks in Saudi Arabia, killing nineteen Americans. There were some anguished words but we did— nothing. It was the same in 1998 when our embassies were bombed in Kenya and Tanzania, killing hundreds. The response was to rearrange some rocks in the Afghanistan desert with a few cruise missiles.

It was the same in October 2000, when suicide terrorists blew a gigantic hole in USS *Cole*, killing seventeen sailors and almost sinking one of the U.S. Navy's most advanced ships.

Like Hamlet, we responded with "words, words, words," and only token military gestures.

In the wake of September 11, it appears that this policy of bellicose vacillation has changed. Still, as of this writing in early 2002, one hears plenty of voices urging not caution but abdication. The left-liberal establishment cannot long bear to see a strong America regnant. It was chastened by disaster but incited by the prospect of losing hold of its illusions. Yet there are also encouraging signs, not least President Bush's State of the Union address at the end of January, that America is prepared to follow through on its promise to eradicate terrorism and hold responsible those states that sponsor, finance, or abet it. In this it is reclaiming a central part of Pericles' vision. "Make up your minds," Pericles said toward the end of his great oration, "that happiness depends on being free, and freedom depends on being courageous. Let there be no relaxation in the face of the perils of the war."

Let me end with a different historical parallel. Among the neglected masterpieces of Victorian political thought is Walter Bagehot's book *Physics and Politics*. Published in 1872, it outlines the requirements for the survival and advance of civilization. Bagehot's ideal is the civilization that he inhabited himself: the liberal democratic polity of nineteenth-century Britain where most disputes were settled in law courts and politics was pursued through discussion, not arms. But Bagehot was canny enough—one might say he was grown-up enough—to understand that such a polity had been made possible in the first instance by force and that it could be maintained in the long run only through the distillates of force that economic might and military prowess represent. "History," Bagehot wrote, "is strewn with the wrecks of nations which have gained a little progressiveness at the cost of a great deal of hard manliness, and have thus prepared themselves for destruction as soon as the movements of the world gave a chance for it."[8] In the context of our discussion here, Bagehot's observation looks like a summary of Pericles' funeral oration, or at least a central part of it. Does Pericles point the way? The alternative is cultural suicide.

8. Walter Bagehot, *Physics and Politics: Or, Thoughts on the Application of the Principles of "Natural Selection" and "Inheritance" to Political Society*, edited with an Introduction by Roger Kimball (Ivan R. Dee, 1998), p. 58.

JAMES BOWMAN

Keen About Death

The Lost Language
of National Honor

"The Americans must know there are thousands of young people
who are as keen about death as Americans are about life."
—Sulaiman Abu Ghaith, spokesman for al-Qaeda
(Quoted in *The Times* of December 28, 2001)

"I wish Ally McBeal and other shows could be there [in
Afghanistan] to show them what the real world is like."
—Alice West, producer of *Ally McBeal*
(Quoted in "Pseud's Corner" of *Private Eye*,
December 28, 2001/January 10, 2002)

DO WE SUPPOSE that "the real world" is more like what we
see on *Ally McBeal* or more like that of al-Qaeda? It is an interesting question because an argument can be made that, for all
the evil committed by Osama bin Laden and his henchmen,
theirs is the world in which most of the human race has lived
for most of its history—a world "keen about death" in all the
areas of life where honor demands it. This is precisely what
contemporary Americans do not and perhaps cannot understand. How is it possible to be "keen about death" without
being deranged? Yet we make a mistake if we regard those parts
of the world that are still obsessed with honor, as our own
ancestors used to be, as being subject to mass psychosis.

For one thing, wars are fought for and about and by means of honor, even though we may no longer use the term. As the events of September 11 have revealed, the honorable response to being attacked, which is to retaliate against and punish the aggressor, is something so natural to the human condition that it takes a very small dose of reality to bring it back even from a very long slumber. We have seen this happen before, most notably after Pearl Harbor when suddenly the debate over the war that had dominated American political discourse fell silent and there was near-unanimity on the need to defend American national honor, even if that meant being "keen about death."

Not that, for the most part, we talked about the "day of infamy" in terms of national honor. The term itself had fallen out of favor after its use to justify the slaughter of the First World War and even then sounded at best old-fashioned, at worst a hypocritical dodge of the cruel and unfeeling. But if we no longer spoke the language of honor, the thing itself was suddenly uppermost in the minds of ordinary people. Now, no more than sixty years ago, do we find it natural to talk about "national honor," however. Although the word "honor" has been often in the mouths of Osama bin Laden and his lieutenants and allies, I have seen the expression only once used by an American: when Rich Lowry, editor of *National Review*, wrote that "For the public, the war on terrorism will probably be about nothing less than national honor, and that is not something that can be finessed or negotiated away in coalition politics." About this, Lowry seems to have been both right and wrong. The American war *was* a matter of national honor, but most Americans were unaware of the fact. Accordingly our leaders preferred to speak in terms of opposing the enemies of our country because of their uniquely heinous "evil" deeds rather than their affront to national honor.

The last time that the word "honor" appeared in the national discourse in anything like its original sense was the occasion on which Richard Nixon announced that his goal in the Vietnam war, which he had inherited from his predecessor, was "peace with honor." It was not Nixon's fault that America's speedy abandonment of its South Vietnamese ally after her own withdrawal from the war made a mockery of that slogan. He had already been dishonored for other reasons by that time and forced from office. But for a quarter of a century after Nixon's retreat to San Clemente (and then to Saddle River) no subsequent president or aspirant to leadership dared to use the word "honor" in any but the vaguest and most innocuous contexts. It was as if honor itself had been dishonored by his disgrace.

Moreover, Nixon's biographer, Stephen Ambrose, has also in the intervening years led the nation in a celebration of the now-aged and dying veterans of the Second World War as "The Greatest Generation" (the title of Tom Brokaw's book) on the grounds of the moral enormities committed by the powers over which they won their victory—as if it were only on that ground that America could claim her moral right to have fought back after being attacked. This historian has thus helped to encourage the mistaken but widespread view that America went to war in 1941 against the evil of Nazism and not in defense of her national honor. It is not coincidental that it is now routine for American presidents to adopt a similar view in justifying military action of any kind—the view that war in general can only be justified in terms of good and evil.

Thus in the wake of the terror attacks on New York and Washington, President George W. Bush duly proceeded to justify retaliation against his country's proclaimed enemies on the grounds not that they were enemies who had challenged America's honor but only because of their unique evil. In doing so he was following the example of his father ten years earlier in characterizing the deeds of the Iraqi dictator, Saddam Hussein, and of his predecessor in the case of Slobodan Milosevic—who was awaiting trial on "war crimes" charges in The Hague at the time when the latest crop of evil-doers revealed themselves over Manhattan, Washington, and Pennsylvania. Ronald Reagan, too, had alarmed many people who feared what they saw as his warlike tendencies in describing the Soviet Union as an "evil empire" in 1982.

Not that his description was not accurate. In the same way, there was plenty of reason for regarding the hijackers and their sponsors, like Saddam and Milosevic, as evil men. But there could be unforeseen adverse consequences to stressing their evil so much that people are not reminded that challenges to the national honor must be resisted whether they come as the result of unequivocal evil or not.

It could be argued, for instance, that it was not the talk of national honor when the nations of Europe went to war in 1914 that produced the postwar letdown whose consequences are still with us today. That was instead a popular response to the experience of having been sold a savage and destructive war after it became no longer tenable to regard the enemy as uniquely evil. As J. C. Squire wrote,

> God heard the embattled nations sing and shout:
> "Gott strafe England" and "God Save the King,"
> God this, God that and God the other thing.
> "Good God," said God. "I've got my work cut out."

In somewhat the same way, the Vietnam war was oversold as being against "the Communists"—presumably the same people as those responsible for the Soviet Gulag and whose armies were then keeping in subjection the nations of Eastern Europe—through fear that the alternative (of keeping South Vietnam in the American rather than the Soviet sphere of influence) smacked too much of old-fashioned "imperialism."

In both these cases, war-weariness after years of slaughter led people eventually to question the moral foundations of the war and to ignore the honorable ones. In 1917 and 1918 it was becoming easier to believe that the Germans, so far from being the moral monsters they were portrayed as being in 1914, were as much as the Allies themselves merely victims of the war, with its muddled "war aims," and the generals and politicians who were seen as keeping it going for sinister reasons of their own. Likewise, by 1968 and 1969, the Vietnamese enemy, the Viet Cong and the North Vietnamese, were looking not at all like agents of some Stalinist bureaucracy but rather worryingly like the gallant freedom-fighters they represented themselves as being. If that was the case, America was no longer fighting an evil empire. It was one.

The kind of romanticism that adopted this view of America's enemy in Vietnam is not quite extinguished even today. The almost reflexive anti-Americanism of many on the Left creates sympathy even for "assymetrical" attacks upon American hegemony by such staggeringly illiberal forces as those of Osama bin Laden. But the careful historian should recognize the central difference between the primitive honor-based culture represented by al-Qaeda and the Taliban and the "progressive" (if misguided) forces that America has been accustomed to opposing since the Second World War. Our new enemies, unlike the old, speak a language that we once spoke and that we might need to learn to speak again.

GUILT VS. SHAME

Anthropologists have long recognized the differences between what they call "guilt cultures" and "shame cultures." Ours is a guilt culture, but like most guilt cultures it has evolved out of a more primitive shame culture of a kind that we still find in many parts of the world, including Afghanistan and other Muslim countries where honor remains of paramount concern among the ruling elites.

In shame cultures it is public behavior and reputation that are all-important. They are dominated by a masculine and military ethos that values above all (for men) bravery in battle, or in the assertion of status—or, to be more precise, the *reputation* for such bravery—and for women the reputation for chastity. A man cannot be shamed even by cowardice, a woman even by unchastity, so long as neither is made public.

We in the more highly evolved guilt cultures of the West may regard such cultural manifestations as primitive, but they are hardly extinct even among us—as the residual potency of such words as "wimp," "meek," or "milquetoast" (as applied to a man) or "slut" (as applied to a woman) suggest. We are ourselves the heirs of a long literary and cultural tradition that accepts and even celebrates the principle embraced, more or less explicitly by Osama bin Laden, namely, that "might makes right."

At some level, we still embrace this principle ourselves. It is fundamental to democracy, for example, since the sheer force of numbers of the majority is deemed by convention to constitute right. Or right enough. War itself represents an implicit acknowledgment that we believe (our) might will make right. Looked at in this way, the ancient rules of honor that were formulated on the same principle may not seem quite so anachronistic.

When in days of old men of a certain class were prepared to "call out" each other and fight duels over trivial slights, they were asserting this principle. To kill your opponent in single combat was in effect to establish that you were right. Thus Sir

Launcelot in Sir Thomas Malory's *Mort D'Arthur* insisted on his right to continue his adulterous affair with Queen Guinevere on the grounds that he could defeat in single combat any knight prepared to object to it. There's chivalry for you!

In the Renaissance, the laws of honor were a subject of intense interest and were codified by Castiglione and a host of other, mainly Italian, authors of handbooks of how what amounted to a new class of courtiers were to behave so as to maintain their honor as members of the elite, which was marked out by such honor. The point of such books was to explain, among other things, what classes of insults or injuries could not be endured by a gentleman without resort to combat. The most serious of these, and the most certain to result in a challenge, were imputations against a man's truthfulness or his courage, but there were also a number of forms that such imputations could take. Hamlet, a trained courtier of the period, goes through the list of them in one of his soliloquies:

> Am I a coward?
> Who calls me villain? breaks my pate across?
> Plucks off my beard, and blows it in my face?
> Tweaks me by th' nose? gives me the lie i' the throat
> As deep as to the lungs? who does me this?
> Ha!
> 'Swounds, I should take it: for it cannot be
> But I am pigeon-liver'd and lack gall
> To make oppression bitter, or ere this
> I should have fatted all the region kites
> With this slave's offal . . .

In the twentieth century it became fashionable to say that Hamlet was, in the words of Laurence Olivier's voiceover to his filmed version of the play, "a man who could not make up his mind." But no contemporary of Shakespeare would have seen it that way. From the moment that he learns from the ghost of the murder of his father, Hamlet says, "Haste me to know 't, that I, with wings as swift / As meditation or the thoughts of love / May sweep to my revenge." Of course the irony of wings of thought would have been apparent, but no one would have supposed that Hamlet was debating with himself whether or not he ought to do what in honor any man of the time would have supposed himself obliged to do. His hesitation *might* have been, for the audience as for Hamlet himself, a result of cowardice, but it could hardly have been as a result of his calling into question the entire foundation of masculine honor as it was understood in his time.

This is not to say that Shakespeare himself might not have been calling that foundation into question. But the enjoyment of the play by its Elizabethan or Jacobean audience, like that of the Athenian audience for Aeschylus' Orestean trilogy, depended on what would have been at the time the all-but-universal assumption that Hamlet was obligated in honor to avenge his father's murder, particularly since he had no redress at law against the man who was now king of Denmark. It is true that the obligation in honor to avenge a murdered kinsman was already dying out in Western Europe in Shakespeare's time, because justice was in the process of being nationalized. That's why Sir Francis Bacon described revenge as "wild justice." But the principle of the vendetta has survived into the present day in parts of the world where political and legal authority is weak, including the streets of our major cities.

By the eighteenth century, the honor culture of Western Europe and the emerging American republic only required that a gentleman who had been cuckolded or insulted show himself willing to shoot and be shot at *pro forma* by issuing or accepting a challenge and then allowing his seconds to negotiate with his adversary's. Actual combat rarely resulted. It was enough to prove one's courage by showing one's willingness to face an armed opponent—and occasionally, as in the case of Alexander Hamilton, whom we now venerate as being among the wisest of our Founding Fathers, death would still result.

The Victorians, like ourselves, were somewhat embarrassed by the survival of such primitive behavior into their time, and they finally put an end to the cult of the duel (in Britain and America, though not everywhere on the Continent). But at the same time they recognized that honor and the things it made men do could not simply be abolished. For among the things it made men do was fight in wars, and they were not as yet so advanced as to suppose that wars could be abolished. The result was the revival, as they saw it, of the medieval rules of chivalry in revised and updated form which—whether the rules were actually observed or not—served as the ideal for gentlemanly and soldierly behavior right up until the First World War, when such things began to seem merely quaint.

There were other factors in the discrediting of honor that ensued after that war. Simultaneously with it there were explosions in Europe and America of feminism—which was naturally opposed to the masculine and patriarchal canons of honor that decreed a woman's honor (that is, her chastity) like her person the property of her husband, father, or brother—and of psychotherapy. The latter by its very nature would come to see the individual psyche as supreme and not the social standards to which the individual was subordinated by the demands of honor. In the diagnosis of "shell shock"—or as we now call it "post-traumatic stress disorder"—as much as in the indiscriminate slaughter of the trenches that provoked it, the death knell of honor was sounded. Now the remnants of the honor culture still survive in their pure form only where, at the margins of our society, the law and the social sanctions of mainstream culture are weakest and where all-male cultures are still suffered to exist.

In the world of street gangs, for instance, a violent response (or the threat of a violent response) to insult or injury offered to one's honor—sometimes described as being "dissed"—is probably at least as common as it was among eighteenth-century gentlemen. But the dominant society regards such standards of behavior and value as primitive and unnecessary, something that is probably the product of poverty. It is widely supposed that these devotees of street honor can be educated out of it with the help of "anger management" classes or appeals to economic self-interest. But when we ourselves are dissed, we too are capable of reverting to the privileges of the man of honor, who thinks himself entitled to respond to insult or injury with violence simply for the sake of his honor and irrespective of the moralist's dilemma as to whether he has been attacked by terrorist or freedom fighter.

HONOR FOR POSTMODERNS

But although the language of honor has been almost extinct in our Western culture for nearly a hundred years, the events of September 11 were just the latest reminder that honor itself never entirely disappears. Almost as terrifying as the hijackings was the terror of liberal and progressive-minded people confronted with the specter of an old-fashioned, even primitive form of wild masculinity arisen out of the deserts and mountains of the Far East and still speaking its strange language of honor. Here, for instance, is Osama bin Laden as quoted by Tony Judt in the *New York Review of Books*:

> Our brothers who fought in Somalia saw wonders about the weakness, feebleness, and cowardliness of the US soldier [he said] . . . We believe that we are men, Muslim men who must have the honour of defending [Mecca]. We do not want American women soldiers defending [it]. . . . The rulers in that region

have been deprived of their manhood. And they think that the people are women. By God, Muslim women refuse to be defended by these American and Jewish prostitutes.[1]

The charge of effeminacy is a familiar and ancient cause of quarrel—that is to say, violence—in all honor cultures, though there are doubtless many in ours who could cite as one reason for refusing to respond to Osama's challenge the fact that we would thus be acquiescing in his implied disparagement of women. Like any eighteenth-century gentleman, he obviously meant to be provocative. But it is not as if he and his soldiers do not genuinely believe in our weakness and effeminacy, and regard fighting as an honorable task for men. As one of his young soldiers wrote home to his parents in the context of praying for martyrdom: "My great father, don't be upset, this is the men's task, not the women's, who are sitting in the houses. We will meet each other in paradise. You truly raised your son to be brave, not a coward." A poem recited by Hamza bin Laden, son of Osama, on a videotape purported to have been made in front of a wrecked American helicopter, praised the leader of the Taliban as "our emir Mullah Mohammad Omar, symbol of manhood and pride."

It ought to be but probably is not unnecessary to say that the point of such language is not to be insulting to women but to disparage our manhood. Nor is it coincidental that Peggy Noonan, Maureen Dowd, Camille Paglia, and others have written that manly men are, since the attacks, suddenly "in" again. In the same way, as Bernard Lewis reminded us in the *Washington Post* last September 16, the Japanese belief at the time of the attack on Pearl Harbor was "that the United States,

1. "Osama bin Laden, December 1998, from an interview with al-Jazeera television . . ." Tony Judt, "America and the War," *New York Review of Books*, November 15, 2001, p. 4.

despite its wealth and strength, was unmilitary and indeed cowardly, and would easily be frightened out of Asia." The same idea lay behind the attacks on New York and Washington, and, says Lewis, "the calculation is not at first sight unreasonable. The abandonment of Vietnam, the flight under attack from Lebanon and Somalia, the recent preemptive withdrawal and evacuation [of U.S. Marines from Jordan] because of a (probably planted) intercept indicating a threat of terrorist action, all seem to point in that direction."

We have our own means of slandering the manhood of our enemies—not by a direct accusation of effeminacy but by a sort of passive-aggressive resort to quasi-scientific authority. Thus Robert McElvaine argued in the *Washington Post* that the "religion" that "motivates the Taliban" is not Islam but "insecure masculinity. These men are terrified of women."

Other ways of answering the charge of effeminacy also tend to be psychotherapeutic in origin. To charge our enemy with being crazy serves the double function of making him less than fully human and not a moral agent and making ourselves and our precision-guided ordnance into a therapeutic necessity. We are, as it were, surgeons cutting out a human cancer and not (as we like to put it) on the "level" of those who perform deeds of terror.

To submit someone to such instant psychoanalysis is to humiliate him, irrespective of any scientific merit there may be to the diagnosis. But the subtext—that women are weak and not to be feared—is perhaps not so distant from the very un-P.C. charge of effeminacy as the evolved elites might wish. There is no equivalent back-door method of insulting the enemy when it comes to racial, ethnic, or religious taunting. Although there has historically been little reticence among belligerents when it comes to proclaiming the superiority of their own cultures to those of their enemies, the injudicious comment by Silvio Berlusconi, the Italian prime minister, suggesting such a superiority of Western and Christian culture over Eastern and Islamic culture, was almost universally condemned. It might be all right for our side to claim to be fighting for secular, tolerant, and multicultural government, but pointing out that the theocrats on the other side were none of these things could still get you into trouble.

True, there are good political reasons for being careful about such things, but at the most fundamental level, disparagements of the enemy's religion or culture are hardly meant to be taken more seriously than aspersions cast on his sexual potency. The point of Osama's taunt was just to serve as a reminder of why it is necessary to respond to violence with violence. Because, that is, when you run away from a fight, as we did in Somalia, you encourage your enemy to think you weak and afraid (as the language of honor conventionally—stereotypically, if you are a feminist—regards women as being) and unwilling to defend yourself. He will therefore think himself licensed to attack you again and again until his attacks become intolerable, by which time it may well be too late to do anything about them. This is the iron law of conflict that only wishful thinking can deny. At another level, the challenge is put in words both familiar and shocking: the words of a taunting playground bully. Surely, the more advanced and progressive people among us must be asking themselves, grownups do not have to respond to such a primitive and childish challenge?

Ordinary Americans have less trouble with the playground morality according to which international relations are carried out. Polls suggested that they instinctively felt the need to hit back without having, anymore, much in the way of language in which to describe or justify their feelings. "I don't see that we have a choice," David Harrell of Brownsville, Brooklyn, told the *Washington Post*. "We were attacked and bloodied, and a nation has to defend itself." The popularity of the war and of the soldiers fighting it were only bolstered by the military successes of November and December, which did not depend on any sophisticated adumbration of American "war aims" or even very much confidence that it was a war against "terrorism" and not against Islam.

But the rhetorical prosecution of a war is a serious problem of the elites. Ordinary soldiers, particularly in a professional army, have their own sense of honor, which is largely independent of war aims, and military action was not in any case controversial, except on university campuses. But this does not mean that evidence of a rhetorical gap opening up between our leaders and ordinary people is a matter of no moment.

HONORABLE COWARDICE?

In the immediate aftermath of the attacks, for instance, there was a brief controversy about whether or not the terrorist acts had been "cowardly." President Bush called them so, just as President Clinton had done with the terror attacks on the USS *Cole* and the American embassies in Kenya and Tanzania when he was in office, but others wondered what was cowardly about blowing yourself up for a cause you believed in. Bill Maher, host of "Politically Incorrect" on ABC television, briefly outraged the nation's wounded sensibilities by suggesting that the terrorists had not been cowardly at all while American armed forces *had* been so when they had responded to earlier acts of terrorism by firing cruise missiles, from a long way off, at what may or may not have been places once inhabited by the malefactors. Interestingly, a spokesman for Osama bin Laden, in denying at first that he had been responsible for the attacks, himself said that al-Qaeda would have scorned to have been a party to "such cowardly acts" as the terror bombings.

Leaving aside for a moment the understandable anger, pique, or desire to be provocative of all these speakers, what is there to be said about the bravery or lack of it displayed by the hijackers? How, wrote Celestine Bohlen, in the *New York Times*, could a word meaning "a shamefully excessive fear of danger" (as Webster's defines it) be applied "to the killers who brazenly passed through airport security, coolly boarded four airliners, overpowered the crews and flew straight to their targets and to their own fiery graves. The implication" of such an epithet applied to such people, thinks Miss Bohlen, "is that the masterminds are cowards because they have not taken responsibility for their actions, or that the killers are cowards for selecting helpless victims." But this, she claims, would be to do violence to the meaning of the word, and she calls in for support Jesse Sheidlower, the North American editor of the *Oxford English Dictionary*.

"I don't think from any point of view we could call these perpetrators cowardly," Mr. Sheidlower agrees. "Objectively, you have to say that what they did, while malevolent, was also a very brave act. 'Dastardly,' maybe." But "dastardly," apart from being old-fashioned-sounding, includes within its semantic field the idea of cowardice. Which points up another reason for using the word "cowardly" unmentioned by either Ms. Bohlen or Mr. Sheidlower. This is that such a usage represents a harkening back to the days when violence was regulated—or at least was supposed to be regulated—by rules of honor, also sometimes referred to as a "gentlemanly" code. To strike your enemy in the back, when he is not looking or has not got his armor on or is unprepared to give a counterblow, was thought to be cowardly because only someone would do it who feared being beaten in a fair fight.

This is also why President Bush also used the qualifier "faceless" with "coward." Knightly equals—assuming that we lived, as some people still suppose we once did live, in a chivalrous society—would face each other "like men," with devices on their shields indicating who they are. The elementary sense of fairness involved is still to be found in boxing matches or other sporting events, where play is not commenced until both sides declare themselves ready. But terrorists who skulk in the shadows and strike us when we are not looking would say that it is precisely because they would be beaten in a fair fight by our professional soldiers that they have the right to strike when we are not prepared to respond, and to strike civilians. The whole point of terrorism is that it is the only weapon available to those who would have no chance in a fair fight against an overwhelmingly superior enemy. How else are they to have a chance to seek justice against power that refuses them what they want?

In making such an argument, the terrorists can appeal to the example of all the guerrilla warriors who have been romanticized by the Left and, to a greater or lesser extent, the popular culture during the last half century. Mao. Ho Chi Minh. Fidel. Che. America, even in spite of herself, loves these stories of little bands of the faithful and virtuous who stand up to and who finally defeat mighty and presumptively corrupt empires. It is precisely how we characterize the war that effected our own founding as a nation. In Vietnam it was most likely the shock of suddenly finding ourselves in the role of the evil empire, and our enemies in that of the Founding Fathers, which ultimately made the continuation of that struggle unsustainable. It is not the least of the ironies of the present struggle that terrorist Muslims from the honor culture of the desert depend on the work done by Western popular culture, which they loathe, to romanticize and honor people like themselves and to take away the stigma of the dastard from their deeds.

For in the West, little honor any longer attaches merely to being the mightier warrior, or to using our power to bring order, peace, and good government to troubled and violent regions of the world. We have in the quarter-century since the fall of Saigon very often been inclined to accept the post-honorable view of terrorists as freedom fighters whose murderous behavior is to be sympathetically understood, if not necessarily excused, in the Middle East, South Africa, Central America, and other places where we have declined, often in spite of what seemed to significant numbers of Americans to be in the national interest, to become engaged ourselves. Even now, there are those on the left who would seek to explain or excuse the Arab terrorists of September 11 as men who had no other way in which to express their grievance—a grievance always assumed to be justified by their claims of suffering—against a much more powerful and presumptively oppressive authority or suzerainty.

It is true that this explanation is somewhat stretched in the case of the United States, which exercises no *de jure* authority in the homelands of the terrorists. But there are many academically respectable precedents for their counterargument that American "hegemony" (useful word!) in their region of the world is the *de facto* equivalent of an imperialist power—since local authorities are too timid to resist American economic, diplomatic, and military might in the alleged interests of the aggrieved—and that therefore it is to be as legitimately resisted as George III was by the American colonists 225 years ago. And if their tactics are somewhat different from George Washington's, it is only a reflection of their relative weakness. Terrorism is thus merely an assertion of their right to moral and political autonomy in the only way available to them.

THE NEW PATRIOTISM

Fortunately, there are few Americans outside of university faculties inclined to believe this anymore. The patriotism that has been so much in evidence since the events of September 11 is both new and not new. It is new in its intensity and in the willingness it implies among ordinary people to see their government assume new powers in order to avenge the attack on America. It is not new in that Americans have always been a patriotic people and are periodically awakened by events to renewals of their patriotism. But this particular revival may be different from the revivals that followed Pearl Harbor, say, or the Iranian hostage crisis. On the one hand, the postwar individualism of American society has had few demands made on it since Vietnam—and few were made even then on those who did not actually have family members fighting there. Now the army's recruiting slogan appeals to recruits to become "An Army of One" and our leaders tell us that we can best support the war effort by shopping.

On the other hand, our adversary represents not only Islamic fundamentalism but also the kind of primitive honor-culture from which we have become so remote that even Islamic fundamentalism looks familiar by comparison. When the Arab hijackers struck, they confronted America not only with the first attack by a foreign power upon the continental United States in over a century and a half but also with a challenge to national honor of a sort to which liberal and progressive thinking, accustomed to taking a global view of every problem, had almost taught itself to feel immune.

How easy it has become for "the world's only superpower" to think of itself as the honest broker between Arab and Israeli in the Middle East or nationalist and Unionist in Northern

Ireland or Serb and Muslim in the former Yugoslavia. America could patronize those who were engaged in what it inevitably saw as petty regional squabbles because of her power and wealth, but also because of a liberal and unheroic habit of mind by which she saw herself as not being bound by the same rules of honor that made those disputes so intractable. American mediators and peacemakers (and especially American academics) got into the habit of talking of "the cycle of violence" as if they could scarcely imagine themselves and their country caught up in anything so absurd.

Ordinary Americans, by contrast, found it much more natural to revert to the idea of honor, even if the word itself remained elusive. When the tabloid *Globe* reported (alas, probably inaccurately) that Osama bin Laden had been killed in a U.S. bombing raid on December 15, it claimed that he "met his end whimpering like a coward" and that his comrades "told him to stop complaining and die like a man." It may come as a surprise to those for whom "honor" seems a hopelessly old-fashioned, even primitive concept, that there is still a mass audience in America who can readily understand what it means to "die like a man." For all of our sakes, we should be glad that there is. But is it not also the case that the elites should be reintroduced to this useful terminology? Thus we read in the *Wall Street Journal* that

> If we really intend to extinguish the hope that has fueled the rise of al-Qaeda and the violent anti-Americanism throughout the Middle East, we have no choice but to re-instill in our foes and friends the fear and respect that attaches to any great power . . . .
>
> Only a war against Saddam Hussein will decisively restore the awe that protects American interests abroad and citizens at home. We've been running from this fight for 10 years. In the

Middle East, everybody knows it. We're the only ones deluding ourselves.[2]

"Fear," "respect," "awe"—these are the things that our grandfathers meant by "honor." If we think these are good things for us to have, perhaps we ought to start using the word again as well, and go easier on the insistence, so uncomfortably like our enemy's, that we are fighting a war of good against evil. Nor is our experience in the twentieth century with universal principles as the motivation for political and military action very encouraging. Why are we—rhetorically anyway—so reluctant to fight not as the party of universal peace and justice but simply as Americans, a people under attack?

It seems a fact not entirely unrelated to its language of good and evil that our political culture was convulsed by a wave of hysteria about security that resulted in confiscation of nail files and the like at airport screening stations. An honor culture would regard such excessive concern for safety as a sign of cowardice. Here is something that our leaders could do to show leadership: announce that security will *not* be tightened, but call upon the men of America to be vigilant and to resist aerial terrorists—as in fact the men (and women) of America have been doing on their own and without any exhortations from their leaders, for example on American Airlines flight 63 when Richard Reid tried to set off a bomb in his shoe. Honor means, among other things, not submitting to threats, and an appeal to honor in such a case would not only be remarkably efficacious against hijackers but also contribute to national pride and morale.

For America wins no friends by the kind of moral chauvinism that insists at every turn that she is better than her enemies.

2. Reuel Marc Gerecht, *Wall Street Journal*, December 19, 2001, p. A 18.

In some ways, this is worse than the more familiar sorts of ethnic or religious chauvinism that we so ostentatiously eschew and more likely to inflame the discontented of the world. A poor man will listen with interest and gratitude to a rich man who tells him that he may become as rich as he is, but he will turn away in disgust from a rich man who tells him that he may become as good as he is. Why, in any case, do we cling to what is inevitably seen as a hypocritical insistence on our moral superiority to our adversaries when so much of the world understands at once and instinctively the simple right of a nation under attack to defend itself?

It is an interesting question, that of whence comes this assumption that we occupy a higher moral level than our would-be adversaries—particularly since it so often occupies the minds of those who, in another context, argue forcefully that America's culpable exercise of political, economic, and military power in the world puts her *beneath* the level of that power's innocent victims. Perhaps a counterattack would allow her to *rise* to their level? But among most of those who use such an argument, a natural pride in the achievements in liberalism and tolerance and democracy among the nations of the West allows a degree of neglect of the basic sense in which we are, always have been, and always will be on the same level as those who attack us: the level of being required by the demands of honor to answer a blow with a blow—or a series of blows—or else to sacrifice our self-respect as well as our respect in the world.

JOHN PODHORETZ

Hollywood Searches for a New Script

Popular Culture After September 11

"I WAS TRYING TO KNIT AMERICA
BACK TOGETHER AGAIN"

In early December 2001, the actress Goldie Hawn made an appearance in Washington, D.C. She was there not to promote a movie or to appear at a benefit. Rather, she was delivering a major policy address in a venue designed for such a purpose: a luncheon at the National Press Club. Her topic was not a subject on which Miss Hawn possesses singular expertise—unlike, say, the tribulations of being a movie star in her fifties with a daughter whose career is more successful, the virtues of unmarried cohabitation with Kurt Russell, and the uses of plastic surgery. In all of these matters, Goldie Hawn may be the world's foremost expert.

Her oration dealt with issues of far greater moment. "On September 11, 2001, the world changed," she informed an audience no doubt deeply illuminated by this unexpected observation. Miss Hawn found herself "moved by acts of remarkable courage" she witnessed on that day. She "learned that we are all vulnerable." And, most strikingly, she found that deep within her cleavage, there beat a patriotic heart.

"Even I bought red, white, and blue yarn and knitted an American flag," Miss Hawn said—a noble sentiment, though it's more likely one of her assistants actually purchased the wool. "I think, in my own small way, I was trying to knit America back together again," the actress offered. (This is something else she does know about intimately, having previously united a racially and culturally divided America in common national indifference to films like *Town and Country* and *Housesitter*.)

Now, Goldie Hawn's expression of patriotic fervor was certainly genuine. It was a perfect reflection of the feeling of wounded righteousness that swept across the United States even as the World Trade Center buildings were coming down. It is sad that it should seem remarkable for a mainstream motion-picture performer to make a public display of her love of country. Such displays should be constant, given the nature of the lives led in the world of show business. The American celebrity class is living out the American meritocratic dream (in a highly exaggerated version, to be sure). Performers have almost always been born in modest circumstances and yet have managed in the space of only a few years to rise to the apex of wealth, fame, and power—due entirely to personal qualities and not to conditions of birth or class.

But the Hollywood affect for three decades or more has been to bask in the glories and wealth of the United States while evincing deep concern about the supposed inequities and injustices suffered by her citizens and others abroad. After all, what good is cultural power if it doesn't buy you the right to instruct others less fortunate than you on what to think and how to act?

"In a post–September 11 world, we need to worry less about being clever and more about being wise," Goldie Hawn told the National Press Club audience. "We need to realize that each person has his or her own unique, special soul print. And every soul and every body deserves to be spoken to with care and respect."

Now, more than ever, we must learn to discourse nicely: "We used to pretend that we didn't care when someone said something unkind. We would say, 'sticks and stones will break my bones, but names will never hurt me.' But words do hurt, and painful words have no place in our better normal world."

No one knows this better, in Miss Hawn's view, than an extremely famous and rich person: "Every actor, everyone in public life, has experienced the pain that gossip and untruths can cause." So she has joined with Rabbi Irwin Katzof in a national campaign entitled Words Can Heal to "combat verbal violence and gossip."

Miss Hawn acknowledges that some may be pessimistic about the efficacy of her efforts. "You think Americans can't reduce gossip and verbal abuse? Does it sound impossible? It's not." After all, "there was a time when slavery was considered normal in America."

How exactly does all this relate to September 11? In Miss Hawn's view, "negative words" are weapons of soul destruction. "They can tear us down or terrorize us," she says. "Negative words can hurt us for the rest of our lives—words like 'I hate you,' 'fatty,' 'loser' or even the new word of war, 'infidel.'" Thus has Goldie Hawn achieved a remarkable Hegelian synthesis. The *National Enquirer* and Osama bin Laden emerge from the same dark wellspring. Calling someone "fatty" is comparable to enslaving him.

Now, I acknowledge that I have, in the preceding ten paragraphs, waged what Goldie Hawn and her rabbi might consider a campaign of "verbal violence and gossip" against her. I am sure that if she read these words, her feelings would be bruised. Still, what I have not done is "terrorize" her. There is a vast distinction between subjecting someone to ridicule and invoking in him a deep, mindless, primal fear.

And there is an even greater distinction—a distinction both practical and moral—to be drawn between the pain caused by gossip and the pain caused when three airplanes crash into three occupied buildings and one crashes into a Pennsylvania field. Given the 10,000 American casualties (both dead and injured) from the al-Qaeda attacks, one might think even a Hollywood celebrity might be reticent about using them as a way of giving her own solipsistic concerns a scope and seriousness they do not deserve.

The fact that Goldie Hawn did not show any such reticence is revelatory—not about her own character so much as the nature of present-day American popular culture.

"MAYBE I SHOULD WATCH MY DIET"

Weekly following September 11, some major pop-culture figure stuck his expensively pedicured foot in a mouth filled with expensively capped teeth trying to say something meaningful about the events.

Barbra Streisand told *USA Today*: "I can't explain it, but I had a feeling something was coming. And then, oh, my God, it's here, this nightmare, this horror. One day I tell myself, 'Screw everything, I'm getting a Carl's Jr. hamburger and eating fried chicken three nights in a row. I don't care about my weight.' The next day, my optimistic side takes over and I think, 'Wait a minute, life goes on, people will get wiser, justice will prevail. Maybe I should watch my diet.'"

The very personal solipsism of Hawn and Streisand was matched by the professional solipsism of film director Robert Altman. He could not imagine that Osama bin Laden might have been engaged in other activities—like joining the mujahedin in Afghanistan, plotting against the Saudi royal family, and following an Islamic-fundamentalist faith enjoining graven images of any kind—that might have precluded his regular attendance at the cinema. In an interview with a British newspaper, Altman declared that "the movies set the pattern, and [the terrorists] have copied the movies. Nobody would have thought to commit an atrocity like that unless they'd seen it in a movie."

Richard Gere, who practices Tibetan Buddhism when he isn't rolling his eyes into his head to express his pain and sorrow on screen, offered his best wishes for the karma of the terrorists. "It's all of our jobs to keep our minds as expansive as possible," said the star of such mind-expanding entertainment as *Autumn in New York* and *Mr. Jones*. "If you can see the terrorists as a relative who's dangerously sick and we have to give them medicine, and the medicine is love and compassion. There's nothing better."

These sorts of remarks put one in mind of Wittgenstein's final proposition in *Tractatus Logico-Philosophicus*: "Whereof one cannot speak, thereof one must be silent." Just because celebrities are asked their views of the changing world circumstances does not mean they are required to offer those views up for general consumption.

The purpose of celebrity is to garner attention. A news event garners attention; therefore, a celebrity gravitates to it in the hopes of diverting some of that attention his way. Sometimes a celebrity will be elevated by a display of genuine self-sacrifice. That was the case for some stars (Jim Carrey, Tom Hanks) in the aftermath of September 11, who quietly donated $1 million of their own money to relief efforts. But more often, the news event is to the celebrity as a glowing bug zapper is to a fly—alluring, hypnotic, irresistible, and deadly.

MODESTY AND CELEBRITY

It has been nearly impossible for any of us to put into words the cluster of emotions brought up by September 11 or by the sight of Ground Zero. As a result, we resort to default words and phrases: "It's unbelievable," or "I wish it were September 10," or "It's just so sad."

These default phrases speak to the essential modesty with which most of us approached this enormous event in the first three months. Even intellectuals and pundits, always ready to express an opinion about the causes of any calamity and a program to address it, were cowed. Were the attacks the result of an intelligence lapse? Inattention on the part of current and previous administrations? Islamic fundamentalism run amok? An outgrowth of the Israeli-Palestinian problem? The answer to all of these questions was, quite simply, *we don't know yet.*

What's more, it seemed that rushing to answer them might even be irresponsible. The search for these answers would have required us to turn inward and examine our own failings at a moment when the nation needed to keep its eyes focused on an outside enemy. There would be time enough to point fingers and study the record. It did not have to happen in the first three months.

Modesty in the expression of controversial opinion is not to be expected from pundits and intellectuals. Still, with very few exceptions, they rose to the challenge.

But if there can be said to be an elite even less modest than the intellectual elite, it would have to be the show-business elite. Several of the latter elitists found it all too easy to draw large lessons from a little knowledge.

Writer-director Oliver Stone's very name has become short-hand for a worldview in which the American government is responsible for every ill on the planet. He is considered a bit loopy in Hollywood, but he is also the only working filmmaker to have won four Academy Awards, and so it can't be said that his opinions are outside his industry's mainstream. At a panel discussion sponsored by the New York Film Festival just weeks after the attacks, Stone launched into a tirade about how the six conglomerates that own movie studios—which is to say, the six businesses he knows—"have control of the world. They control culture, they control ideas. And I think the revolt of September 11 was about, 'F*** you! F*** your order.' The Arabs have a point."

His fellow panelist Christopher Hitchens reared in disgust at Stone's use of the word "revolt," and the views Stone expressed would be equally revolting to 90 percent of Americans. But there's little question that a significantly larger number of people in show business probably share Stone's general outlook, though they might have better timing and more self-control than he.

The central aspect of the Oliver Stone worldview is its simplicity. Whatever the world's problems, they all have their origin in a military-industrial-intelligence-corporate complex that killed John Kennedy, involved us in Vietnam, got Richard Nixon elected, created the junk bond, and went to war with

Iraq for oil and Saudi Arabia. It's the philosophy of Walt Kelly's comic strip, "Pogo": "We have met the enemy, and he is us."

"IN THE FIFTIES, THERE WAS A BLACKLIST"

Others in Hollywood look at America and say, "We have met the enemy, and he is *them*"—and by them, they don't mean Osama bin Laden. Consider the post–September 11 work and comments of Aaron Sorkin, the most celebrated creative talent working in network television today. Sorkin wrote a special episode of his program, *The West Wing*, in which a group of high school students are delivered an hour-long tutorial on Islam and tolerance by the tolerant White House staff—even as the chief of staff is elsewhere in the building grilling a Muslim staff member who shares the same name with an Arab terrorist. Needless to say, the Muslim staff member is not a member of al-Qaeda. The White House chief of staff tells him to get back to work.

Sorkin's great, publicly expressed fear is not for his nation's safety or the challenge of defeating terrorism, but rather the American reaction to it. Following the public outcry against a snotty remark by television chat-show host Bill Maher (who's still on the air, by the way) and the news that two journalists (out of more than 100,000 people who make their living working for American publications) had been fired for writing material deemed insufficiently supportive of the war or the president, Sorkin appeared on a panel in Los Angeles and spoke against a looming evil. "We've heard this song before, right?" he said. "In the fifties, there was a blacklist, and it ruined lives."

Whereupon Sorkin turned into a Pastor Martin Niemoller of the New Millennium, complete with a "when they came for Bill Maher, I did not speak" trope: "If you're anything like me, when you watch any of the dozens of films that have been made about the blacklist, you look at that and think, my God, if I could only transport myself back in time to this period and knock a few heads together and say, are you out of your mind? Well, we're there, right now."

The instinctive reaction among show people is to turn any event into a mirror through which they can continue to pay the most attention to their own reflections. The Emmy awards were twice postponed, in part because television royalty feared they posed too juicy a target for Osama bin Laden. This was true despite that fact that al-Qaeda had indicated on September 11 it was after far bigger game—the world financial system and the American government.

But it was unimaginable to people in Hollywood that they were not next—for don't they produce the very cultural exports that make Osama bin Laden hate the United States? Actually, no. What makes Osama bin Laden hate the United States is democracy, freedom, and Judeo-Christian values. It's mostly leftist academics like Benjamin Barber who are certain the Muslim world has turned against America because of music videos and sexy movies.

The last thing Hollywood can bear to believe about itself is that it is irrelevant—and the last thing its leading lights can bear to believe is that they do not understand what is happening and have little of moment to say about it. Therefore, they converted the events of September 11 into a melodrama with a familiar and comforting villain. For Aaron Sorkin, it was a blacklist melodrama. Oliver Stone saw the attacks as a noble "revolt" against the corporations who have recently failed to offer financing for some of his ruinously expensive motion-picture projects. Goldie Hawn wants a jihad against gossip. Barbra Streisand is waging a titanic struggle against Carl Jr.'s fried chicken.

To be fair, the show-business community in general joined

in the national celebration of the sacrifices of the firefighters and policemen in New York and Washington, the heroism of the men of Flight 93 who stormed the cockpit and brought the plane to ground, and the conduct of President Bush. But so unused is Hollywood to the notion of celebrating the generosity and openheartedness of Americans and America that it could not do so without adding a cautionary warning. In the world of popular culture, the initial instinct was—at least in part—to view the September 11 attacks less as a threat to the people of the United States that had to be answered with mighty force than as a threat to the Muslim minority in the United States from non-Muslim Americans. Now here was a threat about which there could be unanimous determination to do something.

"WE'RE GOING TO TRY TO DO SOMETHING"

On September 21, ten days after the attacks, all American broadcast networks canceled their prime-time programming to join in a two-hour telethon called "America: Tribute to Heroes." George Bush had just spoken before Congress of "our mission and our moment," turning the aftermath of September 11 into a righteous national cause. This was the moment for popular culture—a moment to speak to and capture a bit of the nation's fragile spirit as only popular entertainers seem to be able to do in our time.

But there was none of Bush's spirit on display in the telethon. "We're going to try to do something," said Tom Hanks in the first spoken words heard by 150 million people. That "something" was a threefold effort. First, a fund-raising appeal that resulted in donations exceeding $150 million. Second, a heartfelt memorial to those who died in the attacks. And last but certainly not least, a heartfelt appeal to Americans not to hurt Muslims.

The telethon had barely begun when the audience was treated to a lengthy film clip of Muslim children saying they were sorry for what had happened, and the tragically impaired Muhammad Ali muttering a condemnation of the attack and speaking in praise of Islam. Later, Julia Roberts insisted: "Please, please, let's love one another. Reach out to each other. Be kind to each other."

The notion that the shell-shocked people of the United States were intending to rise up and slaughter the Muslims in their midst had been belied by the national mood in the previous ten days. In a nation of 281 million people, there were 53 reports of "bias" incidents involving Muslims, with a single fatality involving a turbaned Sikh in Arizona. At the time of the telethon, it was still believed that as many as 10,000 people had died at the World Trade Center. And yet the telethon offered a near equivalence between the dead and the nonexistent danger to the Muslims living in the United States.

That nonexistent danger was so serious, in the eyes of Paramount Pictures CEO Sherry Lansing, that she told *Time* magazine she would refuse to make a movie with a Muslim bad guy—which would seem an odd decision to make only weeks after Muslim bad guys in real life had staged the worst attack on United States soil in 187 years. "You [hear about] these Afghan or Arab children who are getting picked on," she said. "You don't want this to be a country where we do this to innocent people."

To be sure, Hollywood was not alone in its obsession with this notion. It was following along a favored subplot of the American news media. But still, the idea of combating prejudice and hate—as opposed to, say, joining in the muscular anger and resolve offered up by George W. Bush—must have been reassuring in Hollywood. Such an approach represented a re-assuring point of continuity between the new national understanding of the world forced upon Americans by Osama bin Laden and Hollywood's pre-attack understanding of America, its place in the world and what it means to be an American.

The problem is that the two cannot so easily be reconciled, if they can be reconciled at all.

BAD DAVID, GOOD GOLIATH

Since Vietnam cleaved the nation in two, the popular culture has presented a schizophrenic image of the United States. When its movies and television programs are not offering any particular message about American life, they portray a people living in casual luxury who happily take for granted the ease and comfort of their lives.

But when these pop-culture works do attempt to speak directly to the issues undergirding American life, they usually portray a nation whose institutions are at war with its people. Corporations, businesses, politicians, the military, and government officials are unfeeling at best and murderous at worst. They are monolithic and totalitarian.

This image of American life is not simply, as many conservatives would have it, a hangover from the anti-war movement in the 1960s. Hollywood's America is a more ideologically complex place—an amalgam of libertarian sentiment, right-wing anti-bureaucratic theory, and leftist anti-capitalism. These wildly contradictory perspectives do have a single common element: They claim to speak for every ordinary American against those who would oppress him in the pursuit of power.

Hollywood's present-day populism has an added kick to it. It's not simply good guys squaring off against bad guys. The bad guys must also be far more powerful than the good guys—

richer, more numerous and more impersonal. Good may eventually triumph over evil, but it's more exciting if the victory comes against all odds. This perspective animates not only the action movies that are Hollywood's mainstay but the mostly ill-informed political views of the pooh-bahs of the popular culture.

What happened on September 11 radically up-ended the Hollywood worldview. The worst crime ever committed against this nation was the result of an entirely different dynamic. By any reckoning, the United States is Goliath and Osama bin Laden is David. America is the giant, bin Laden the speck. And what America and Hollywood have learned is that David can be evil incarnate while Goliath can be innocent and good.

In the wake of the attacks, Hollywood toyed with various theories about the way it would have to change to fit the new national mood. No more violent films, some said; until it turned out that violent films were flying off the shelves at video-rental stores. No war movies, it was said; until a modest effort called *Behind Enemy Lines* made $19 million in its first weekend in November.

Some of the ways in which Hollywood will be changing in the years to come are already evident. It will, for example, be many years before a man in any type of uniform is cast as a villain. A movie called *The Last Castle* saw to that. Set at a military prison with an evil warden holding the rank of colonel against whom a wonderful and wrongly imprisoned general stages a mutiny/riot, *The Last Castle* opened in October to box-office receipts of only $17 million against production and marketing costs above $70 million.

Dreamworks, the studio that made the picture, tried to sell *The Last Castle* as a deeply patriotic work—even though in the ads designed before September 11 the chief image was of the

American flag hanging upside down. It didn't work, to put it mildly. This effort at retrofitting was an act of desperation, but Hollywood's studios had no choice. With billions of dollars in expenditures and lost revenues on the line, they had and have to try and shoehorn the projects that were in the pipeline into the new national consensus.

It is impossible to say what will emerge anew from our popular culture after September 11—which is to say, the sorts of movies and television shows that will be produced for consumption in late 2002 and throughout 2003 and beyond. But I believe the stark reality of a nation attacked has shaken the popular culture to its foundations. American institutions were the object of the September 11 attacks, and Hollywood is sensing that it can no longer comfortably use them to serve as a standard-issue villain.

The popular culture needs a new plot line.

JOHN CORRY

New York, New York

America's Hero

THE SKY WAS crystalline blue the day it happened, and it stayed that way through Thanksgiving. The leaves turned color, but remained on the trees. Central Park was dappled in red, russet, and gold. It was the loveliest Indian summer New York had seen in years, as if somehow the city was being compensated for the evil that had overtaken it. Indeed you could sit on a bench in Battery Park in the warm afternoon sunshine and look out on the glistening harbor, and even though the rubble was only a few streets away, everything seemed as before. The promise of New York was still intact, and it would remain the world's capital. September 11 had not changed that.

Or so you hoped and truly believed, although you knew everything could not be the same as before. The attack on the World Trade Center had killed nearly 3,000 people. It also had made a city that only recently regained its old exuberance aware of its own vulnerability. The Twin Towers had anchored the skyline at the southern end of Manhattan. New Yorkers might have taken them for granted, although they could never ignore their presence. They had risen up 110 stories each from a perfect square at the base, and then loomed over the city like sentinels. It was unlikely they were ever anyone's favorite buildings, but they had inspired a kind of awe. Seen from a distance, or when flying in over the city, the Twin Towers took on the visual force of the Pyramids. Over the years they had embedded themselves in the city's consciousness, and become its best-known emblem. On September 11, though, they vanished, and in their place were only grave sites. Bodies lay in the Twin Towers' ruins, and so, it seemed, did the city's best hopes for the future.

You must understand now that the business of New York has always been business. The Dutch founded New York as a business enterprise, and commerce has made its heart beat ever since. Some of its glories are made of steel and concrete, solid and visible; others are things of the spirit, aspirations and dreams that can only be felt. But both are shaped by the city's economy, and the attack had left the economy damaged. Just how badly it was damaged, or how long it might take to recover, was difficult to know, but pessimism seemed in order. The Chamber of Commerce and the New York City Partnership, which represents the companies that make up the city's business elite, estimated that 100,000 jobs had been lost in and around the World Trade Center, as well as almost 30 percent of the office space. And in turn, they said, this put "at risk" many of the 270,000 jobs still in place south of Chambers Street. In other words, there would be a ripple effect, and in time it would be felt throughout the city. The city comptroller said there would be $100 billion in economic damage within two years. Moreover, because of the slowing economy and a drop in tax collections, especially those from the big Downtown financial firms, the city's own finances already were in decline before September 11. After September 11, the decline became a free fall. Revenues fell, and expenses climbed, and while the city had been projecting a small surplus, it now saw a $4 billion deficit. How would it meet its needs?

Neither Washington nor New York State was likely to bail the city out. A sympathetic President Bush pledged $20 billion in aid the day after the attack, but then Congress intervened. New York was to get $11.1 billion in emergency aid for the year. Meanwhile the state was having its own problems, and Gov. George Pataki said he wanted $54 billion in federal aid to solve both the state's and the city's problems. No one took that seriously; the $54 billion wish-list was stuffed with pork. But it did make clear that for the most part the city would have to fend for itself. It might get reimbursed for its huge cleanup and security expenses, but then it would be on its own.

RUDOLPH GIULIANI'S REAL ACCOMPLISHMENT

But outwardly at least, Rudolph Giuliani and Michael Bloomberg, New York's outgoing and incoming mayors, respectively, seemed confident. The city is "alive and well and open for business," Bloomberg proclaimed after he was elected. He won because of September 11. Only days before the election he had been expected to lose. He trailed his Democratic opponent, Mark Green, in the polls, and was no more than a blur to most voters. He had founded Bloomberg, the financial-information service, and was very rich. He had become a Republican because he thought the Democrat mayoral primary would be too crowded. Just what he would do, or try to do, if he were elected mayor was mostly unknown, although in his speeches, which he gave with a Boston, not a New York, accent, he said there should be less state intervention in city affairs, and that business development should be encouraged. But none of this was likely to grip voters, and as Green said of Bloomberg, possibly correctly, "When he's been to all the neighborhoods like I have, perhaps he'll be slightly more insightful and credible."

Nonetheless Bloomberg won. He had spent $69 million of his own money on the campaign, or $92 or so for each voter, and been endorsed by Rudy Giuliani, but more important, he wasn't Mark Green. When New York finally focused on the election, it found him wanting. He was a casualty of the terrorist attack. The Democratic primary was supposed to be held September 11, but it was suspended in mid-morning, and the mayoral campaign disappeared from front pages and evening news broadcasts. When it reappeared a few weeks later it was only to remind the heavily Democratic city of the local Democratic Party's infinite capacity for racial warfare. Fernando Ferrer, the Bronx Borough president, Green's principal challenger in the rescheduled primary, talked of "two New Yorks." The Green campaign said that was a racial appeal: Ferrer was trying to divide the city by appealing to blacks and other Latinos. After Green won the primary, Ferrer said that Green had been racist. For one thing, he had used an ad that questioned Ferrer's competency, and asked, "Can we afford to take a chance?" And that, Ferrer and his campaign manager said, was a racial appeal. They demanded a recount of the vote, and complained to the Democratic National Committee about Green's supposedly unfair tactics. Even Bloomberg got involved, although it was unlikely many people noticed. He said that he himself would never have run the ad that questioned Ferrer's competency, and demanded to know why Green did.

Meanwhile fires still burned at the World Trade Center—they would not be completely extinguished until the week before Christmas—and the air was still acrid over Downtown Manhattan. Bodies, or parts of bodies, were being pulled from the ruins, and there were funerals for lost firemen and police officers every day. New York had seen disasters before, but never anything like this, and when it finally focused on the election, the only question was, who would best help it to recover? In the ten days before the election, Green's poll numbers declined. Television ads in which Giuliani praised Bloomberg were responsible in part, but equally important, New York was at last paying attention. Green, the city's public advocate, had impeccable liberal credentials. He had begun his career with Ralph Nader, and been a champion of good causes ever since. If Giuliani had left office before his term was up to run for the Senate, Green would have become mayor. Under law, the public advocate, a kind of civic ombudsman, was next in the line of succession, and Green seemed to think this somehow entitled him now. His sense of self-worth was apparent; his manner was somewhat aloof. In earlier years that probably would have been interpreted as proof of his commitment to high principle. September 11, however, changed how New York saw things. Traditional liberal credentials, no matter how impeccable, declined in value, and rather than being an asset they seemed more likely to be a hindrance. At best they were an irrelevance. Sterner qualities were needed in a city that must deal with a crisis, and if New York could not re-elect Giuliani— barred by law from running for a third term—it certainly would not elect Green, the candidate who was most unlike him. Green still had his backers—the *New York Times*, for one, supported him and not Bloomberg—but to most of the city, its middle classes especially, he seemed like a man from the past, trailing useless baggage behind him.

Giuliani, of course, had inspired the city and much of the rest of America. A Time-CNN poll in December found that 90 percent of all Americans thought that the way New York had responded to the terrorist attacks had helped to rally the country; 94 percent said Giuliani had done either a "very good" or a "good" job in providing leadership. *Time* chose Giuliani as its "Person of the Year," and said that his performance after September 11 "ensures that he will be remembered as the greatest mayor in the city's history, eclipsing even his hero, Fiorello LaGuardia. . . . Giuliani's eloquence under fire has made him a global symbol of healing and defiance." Even the *Times* praised his performance after September 11. It said the crisis had brought out the best in him, and that he had shown a side of his character he had not shown before. The crisis in fact had brought out the best in Giuliani; the man and the moment had met, and he had been the true voice of New York.

Still, the strengths and virtues he showed after the terrorist attack were much the same ones he had shown before it. The *Times* and most of the city's elite, however, had not recognized them then for what they were, and had seen in them instead something unattractive and even menacing. It was mostly a visceral reaction. Giuliani, the grandson of Italian immigrants, was born in Brooklyn, and had attended parochial schools. Four of his uncles were cops, and one was a Fire Department captain. But another uncle, kept at a distance by Giuliani's father, was a mob-connected loan shark. When Giuliani was young he thought he might become a priest, but when he grew up he went into law enforcement. He was a product of his background, and he was just not the *Times*'s kind of man.

Separate now the paper's news coverage of the terrorist attack from its oracular editorial pronouncements. The coverage was splendid, and made the *Times* a leading contender for a Pulitzer Prize when the Pulitzers were next to be awarded. But the editorial pronouncements, as they often do, reflected a city of the *Times*'s own making. When most of New York hoped that Giuliani would find a way to waive the rules that kept him from a third term, and even West Side liberals were writing in his name on Democratic primary ballots, the *Times* said it was only Republicans who wanted him to run again. Nonetheless the editorials have their uses; they record a way of thinking. The *Times* listens to the city's elites, and the elites listen to the *Times*, and on municipal matters they speak as one. Their views on Giuliani and how New York should be governed may be found in the paper's editorials.

New York in the 1980s was the poster city for liberal politics gone sour. Crime was up, municipal services were down, and the sound of the city was a car alarm at two in the morning. The city needed a new leader, someone not associated with the old regime. But in 1989, when Giuliani, then U.S. attorney for the Southern District of New York, ran for mayor, the *Times* supported his opponent, David Dinkins. Giuliani, it feared, was a Reagan Republican. He might also be "harsh and moralistic." However, Dinkins, "warts and all," was a "known quantity," and a "practical Democrat." And as New York's first black mayor, he would "instill a sense of pride and participation in blacks and other minority groups."

Dinkins won, and in 1993 the *Times* again supported him over Giuliani, although it needed a torturous editorial almost twice as long as the 1989 one to do it. New York was in an even steeper decline than before, and race relations were worse than ever. Gloom was palpable, and the city seemed resigned to its own decay. Obviously New York was in crisis, but try as the *Times* did, it was unable to explain the crisis away. Instead it attacked Giuliani. It said he was "a man of harsh attitudes," who was "prone to lurching behavior," and that at a police rally he had once used "barnyard language." The election, the *Times* said, was about "values," and if you understood that, you knew that Dinkins was "clearly the more worthy" candidate.

But Giuliani won, and his "values" turned out to be healthier for New York than those of the *Times* or any of his other equally precious critics. He had promised to improve the "quality of life," and he did. The change was almost immediate. Squeegee men and panhandlers seemed embedded in city life; so did welfare cheats and deadbeats. The unacknowledged assumption was that any attempt to remove them would be mean and undemocratic. But the squeegee men went first, and the cheats and deadbeats were not far behind them.

Meanwhile New York, once the butt of late-night television jokes, became the safest big city in America. Neither demographics nor a booming economy, or any combination of the two, could explain why its crime rate dropped as sharply as it did. But soon after becoming mayor, Giuliani told the police department that the incidence of crime—the number of shootings, say, or robberies—mattered more than arrests did. When the incidence rates rose in any of the city's seventy-three precincts, he wanted to know why. Often he would call precinct commanders himself. Soon parks and public places began to fill up with families and children, and not panhandlers and junkies. Neighborhoods were revitalized, tourism was revived, and the city regained its old confidence. It was morning again in New York.

Consequently the *Times* surrendered in 1997, and endorsed Giuliani over his weak Democratic opponent, although it still had reservations. It recognized many of his accomplishments, but said he still had to learn to control himself. He had a "combative temperament," and his "pugnaciousness" was unattractive. But if Giuliani had not been combative and pugnacious, he would not have been able to turn New York around. Blight would have spread, confirming the fear that the city was ungovernable, and that there was an inevitability about its decay. If there had been a terrorist attack under those conditions, it would have had a far more devastating effect than the one on September 11. A dispirited New York would have been without the emotional resources and resilience it needed to recover. But no one wrote the city's obituary after September 11, and as admirable as Giuliani's performance was then, he had done his most important work long before that. He had restored New York's self-confidence, and given it the strength to cope. He had shown it how to deal with a crisis.

NEIGHBORHOOD VALUES

But what if calamity should strike again? In November a jetliner broke apart after taking off from Kennedy Airport and plunged into Rockaway Beach in Queens, a neighborhood already mourning the deaths of some 80 residents lost at the World Trade Center. Meanwhile all 251 passengers on the jetliner died. Most were Dominicans by birth, and New Yorkers by adoption. The city was stricken, and the *Daily News* put out a special edition with a single word on the front page: "Why?" The meditation inside began: "In the depths of his despair, the biblical Job pondered a question for the ages, 'Why do the just suffer and the wicked flourish?' New Yorkers could be forgiven for wondering if God was testing them yesterday after the city endured its second cataclysm since September 11." The *News* is a tabloid, and tabloids sing the songs of the city. If God was testing New Yorkers, then He knew they would somehow survive. There has always been a grittiness to life in New York. It comes from cramming too many people into too small a space, and then insisting they all get along, and while the remarkable thing is that they more or less do get along, there is always some tension. Out-of-town visitors may experience this as rudeness or coldness, but it is really the restless, nervous energy that courses through the city and makes it unlike anywhere else. New York is an idea as much as a place, and whatever its discomforts, people live there by choice. In a way, adversity becomes them.

A month before the attack, a New York Times-CBS News poll asked New Yorkers whether they thought the city would be a better or worse place in which to live in ten or fifteen years: 34 percent said it would be better, and 25 percent said it would be worse; 32 percent said it would be the same. But in a similar poll a month after the attack, 54 percent said that in ten or fifteen years the city would be a better place in which to live, while only 11 percent said it would be worse; 26 percent said it would be the same. The poll the month before the attack also found that 59 percent of New Yorkers thought life in the city had improved in the previous four years. In the second poll, taken the month after the attack, even as smoke still rose from the World Trade Center, 69 percent said they thought life had improved. No doubt that was an expression of defiance, but there was something else, too. September 11 had been horrendous, but it had also awakened a new appreciation of the city.

Much has been made about how the attack left New York steeped in shock, but not enough about how quickly it began to recover. New York was probably better able to cope with what happened September 11 than any other city on earth. Mindful of the 1993 terrorist bombing of the World Trade Center before he became mayor, Giuliani created the Office of Emergency Management soon after he was elected. Disaster scenarios were drawn up, and emergency procedures established for potential calamities. Some of them went into effect on September 11. Ambulances were at the World Trade Center, for instance, only minutes after the terrorists struck. No one, however, had envisioned hijacked airliners flown into skyscrapers, and when the first airliner struck 1 World Trade Center, the North Tower, it seemed possible a terrible accident had taken place. But eighteen minutes later, the second airliner hit 2 World Trade Center, the South Tower, and New York knew it was under attack. In the next hour both towers collapsed. The buildings at 3, 4, 5, 6, and 7 World Trade Center fell later, and sixteen acres of Manhattan were covered with more than one million tons of twisted steel and burning rubble. "I don't know what the gates of hell look like," a man who escaped from one of the towers said, "but it's got to be like this."

When the towers fell they disintegrated into a thick gray cloud that sped outward over the streets, and choked the air with dirt. Hundreds of thousands of office workers fleeing the disaster area had to trudge through the cloud on foot. Some were injured, and many were in shock, and almost all were preternaturally quiet. There was fear and uncertainty, of course, but no widespread panic, and it was much the same way throughout the city. A hush fell over New York, and people walked the streets. Only the day before they would have avoided eye contact, but now they sought it out. Clumps of people formed and re-formed, and asked one another what they had heard. Strangers stopped strangers who looked bereaved, and asked if they could help them. Food banks were started, and clothing drives begun. Blood-donor volunteers were so numerous on September 11 that hospitals had to turn most away; they did not have the facilities to receive them.

Meanwhile the city at large was in stasis, with bridges and tunnels closed, airports shut down, and buses and subways disrupted; but neighborhoods kept functioning, and the neighborhoods are the bones and sinews of the city. The fabled and celebrated people of New York do not as a rule live in those neighborhoods, but ordinary people do, and life there is not the same as it is in, say, the East 60s or the West Side of Manhattan. To be sure, they are neighborhoods, too, and the city would be poorer without them. They give New York cachet, along with its most advanced thinking. But death and destruction demand a utilitarian response, and not advanced thinking. On September 11 the city was reclaimed by the people from the other neighborhoods. They rescued New York physically, and then their values sustained it.

Flags flew everywhere after the attack. They were also hung from apartment and office buildings, and fastened to street signs, automobile antennas, and park benches. There were flag decals on city buses. If you looked south from Fifth Avenue and 42nd Street, you saw the cloud of smoke over what had been the World Trade Center, but if you looked to the north you saw flag after flag, all the way to Central Park. Granted that flying a flag may be an empty gesture, or—remember this was New York—perhaps no more than a fashion statement. Oscar de la Renta put flag decals on his models when he had his winter showing. Other designers did much the same. Nonetheless the patriotic feeling that swept New York was real. When the City Opera opened its season four days after the attack, the entire company came on stage. The company's artistic director asked the audience to stand for a moment of silence, and then join in singing "The Star-Spangled Banner." The audience did, and people cried. At Broadway shows, audiences sang "God Bless America." At the Central Synagogue on Lexington Avenue, the congregation sang "My Country 'Tis of Thee" during Rosh Hashanah.

For the city had suffered a terrible wound, and New Yorkers found solace in expressing a love for their country. In a way, they were also rejoining their country. The glory of New York— the idea of New York—is that millions of people of all colors, beliefs, and nationalities can live in one big city while they pursue their dreams and raise their families, and not get in one another's way. So you may think of New York as representing the best of America, although there have long been suspicions that it is really not a part of America at all. It is too decadent and too international, and it dismisses both traditional patriotism and the old-fashioned manly virtues. The heartland is supposed to be a very long distance away.

But that was before the flags flew and people cried when they sang the National Anthem, and in fact the heartland had never been as far away as anyone thought. It had always been there in the neighborhoods. After September 11, the city's Board of Education passed a unanimous resolution requiring all public schools to lead their students each day in the Pledge of Allegiance. In the past, New York's schoolchildren had always recited the pledge, although in the sixties the practice had waned. At public schools in Manhattan, it seems, the pledge was no longer recited at all. But the old ritual had stayed on at many schools in the outer boroughs. The children there still began their day with the pledge, and often they sang "My Country 'Tis of Thee."

HEROES OF OUR TIME

The 343 firemen and 23 police officers who gave their lives on September 11 apparently went to schools like that; certainly their children do now. Most had lived in the outer boroughs or the family-friendly towns on Long Island or in New Jersey. A disproportionate 78 of the 343 firemen had lived on Staten Island. With only 440,000 people, it is the least populated of the boroughs; it is also the one furthest removed culturally from the rest of the city. Friendships are built around clubs, schools, and churches—a Catholic high school there lost 23 alumni, about half of them cops or firemen—and alone among the boroughs it consistently votes Republican. Every so often, even if not seriously, Staten Island threatens to secede from New York.

On September 11, however, policemen and firemen, the

firemen especially, of course, became New York's heroes. They had gone unhesitatingly into a dangerous place, and given their own lives while trying to save the lives of others. At a very dear and almost unbearable cost the city learned anew an old lesson. "One fireman stopped to take a breath, and we looked each other in the eye," a man who had made it to safety from the 86th floor of the North Tower said later. "He was going to a place I was damn well trying to get out of. I looked at him thinking, 'What are you doing this for?' He looked at me like he knew very well—'This is my job.'"

Yes, it was a job, and it was also a way of life that had been preserved despite the pressures to change it. The Fire Department has a distinct culture. Many firemen are Irish-American or Italian-American, and many had fathers and uncles in the department before them. Officially they are referred to now as firefighters, although the old-fashioned and presumably chauvinistic word, firemen, is more descriptive. The 343 firemen who died on September 11 were, in fact, all men. In a high-tech age, battling fires and rescuing people is still a low-tech operation. Physical strength and endurance are essential, and the Fire Department has had to resist the ministrations of advanced thinking. Some twenty-five years ago, when the Police Department set out to recruit more women and members of minorities, it said it would never lower entrance standards. The political culture, however, determined otherwise; the Police Department had to be more inclusive. Short, fat police officers—short, fat female officers, especially—are not at all uncommon now in New York.

But the Fire Department went on as before. Meanwhile firemen from around the country recognized the New York firemen as special; they came from all over on St. Patrick's Day to march with them in the Fifth Avenue parade, and testify to their legendary courage. New York, by contrast, respected the firemen, but did not think much about them. New Yorkers could identify the police commissioner, but the fire commissioner was anonymous. Actually that was just as well. There was less pressure on the Fire Department to change its ways, and the bonds that knit the firemen together were allowed to stay intact. New York learned about that on September 11. Among the 343 firemen who died were 21 chiefs, 20 captains, and 47 lieutenants. They had led from the front, and the rank and file had followed. This was tragic and valorous; it was also inspiring. New York had found true heroes.

Meanwhile, that day and the next, homemade flyers with pictures of missing people went up on walls, kiosks, and subway and bus stops all over the city. "Have you seen this person?" the flyers asked. Surely some of those listed as missing had been hospitalized, or perhaps they had wandered away in shock. They could not all be dead; there had to be survivors, but even if there were none, there would still be bodies for burial. There would be solace in the rituals for mourning.

So the flyers described the missing people in only the most general way—height and weight, and perhaps eye or hair color—and that was thought to be enough. But by the end of the week the terrible reality had taken hold, and new flyers went up on the walls and kiosks. They described the missing people in more intimate detail, and even told something about their lives. One of the missing, for example, was "a wonderful father and husband." A picture, apparently taken at a backyard cookout, showed him with two small children. They all wore matching aprons. Another flyer showed an attractive young woman, last seen, it said, on the 95th floor of Tower One, wearing "a light green necklace, wedding ring with Nick on the inside, and a bracelet watch." An older woman was said to have had a "little scar at the center of forehead, and a mole at the jawbone near right ear." Meanwhile a man, shown smiling as he sat behind the wheel of a car, had worn "a silver wedding band and silver watch on left hand." Another man, presumably young, had "braces on his teeth."

The men and women in the flyers were, of course, all dead, and the inclusion of the small details meant that their families recognized now that their bodies would never be recovered. But a light green necklace or a silver wedding band might help to identify the remains. Many of the families, however, would be denied even that small comfort. The explosive force of the attack had obliterated bodies, and identifying them was virtually impossible. On the other hand, there was always hope, and teams of police detectives were combing night and day through the sad rubble from the World Trade Center that was carried in trucks to a landfill on Staten Island. This was backbreaking work in what seemed to be an unpleasant place. The air was foul, and methane gas bubbled up from the ground. The detectives, many of them volunteers, had to wear protective suits to guard against contamination. Visitors to the site, though, were impressed by their determination. If there was anything in the rubble that might help comfort the grieving families, surely they would find it.

The scene at what was once the World Trade Center was quite different. Ground Zero had become a tourist attraction. At first the city had tried to keep visitors away. Tarpaulins were hung on chain link fences all around the devastated area to discourage people from coming by and staring. The sad and holy place was not to be a spectacle; it demanded a feeling of reverence, and it was not to be commercialized. But by year end the tarpaulins had come down, and the fences were moved closer to the crash site. The city even erected wooden platforms on which tourists could stand and get the best views. This may seem inconsistent with the earlier desire to keep people away, but it really was not. The tourists would also spend money and stimulate commerce, and in New York's way of thinking there was no reason at all that this should be incompatible with feeling reverence. New York, as always, would be a place where money and dreams could meet, and a terrorist attack would not change that.

CONTRIBUTORS

ANNE APPLEBAUM is an American journalist based in London and Warsaw. She contributes regurarly to the *Sunday Telegraph* and *Slate*, and is completing a history of the Soviet Gulag.

JAMES BOWMAN is American editor of the *Times Literary Supplement* and media critic for *The New Criterion*.

JOHN CORRY is a former *New York Times* reporter and media critic and the author of *My Times: Adventures in the News Trade*.

ROGER KIMBALL is managing editor of *The New Criterion*. His books include *Experiments Against Reality*, *The Long March: How the Cultural Revolution of the 1960s Changed America*, and *Tenured Radicals: How Politics Has Corrupted Higher Education*.

DANIEL PIPES is director of the Philadelphia-based Middle East Forum, columnist for the *New York Post* and *Jerusalem Post*, and author of *Conspiracy* (Free Press).

WLADYSLAW PLESZCZYNSKI, former executive editor of the *American Spectator*, is a distinguished visiting fellow at the Hoover Institution and editor of *TheAmericanProwler.org*. He has written for the *Wall Street Journal*, *Weekly Standard*, *Times Literary Supplement*, and *Women's Quarterly*.

JOHN PODHORETZ is a columnist for the *New York Post* and a contributing editor of the *Weekly Standard*.

BYRON YORK is White House correspondent for the *National Review*. His writing has also appeared in the *American Spectator*, the *Atlantic Monthly*, the *Wall Street Journal*, and the *Weekly Standard*.

INDEX

Afghan-Pakistani border; patrolling of, 4

Afghanistan, American air campaign in, 48–51; funding education in, 17; international investigation of terrorist financing in, 3; United States fighting in, 16

airplanes, box cutters on, 28; knives on, 28; marshals on, 28

airports, screening stations in, 102; security in, 30

al-Jazeera, Arabic-language satellite television station, 18

al-Qaeda network, 6; funding of terrorist groups by, 15; growth of, 17; United States and, 22–23, 56–57

Albright, Madeline, 2

Ali, Muhammad, 113

Altman, Robert, 107

Ambrose, Stephen, 83

American(s), air campaign in Afghanistan by, 48–51; dehumanizing of, 43; fatalities, 43; patriotism of, 98–101; reaction to terrorism by, 110. *See also* United States

Amtrak, 35

Annan, Kofi, 5

anti-terrorism, measure, 22; money for, 33

Arab media, bin Laden, Osama, and, 52

Arafat, Yasser, 42; Sharon, Ariel, on, 13

Arendt, Hannah, 64, 65

Aristotle, 67

Ashcroft, John, 36; list of proposals by, 23

Aviation and Transportation Security Act, 21, 22, 28–31

aviation security bill, 22

Bagehot, Walter, 79
baggage area, security in, 30
baggage screeners, federalizing of, 28–31
Balkans, *ad hoc,* development of, 2; peace-keeping operations in, 1
Barber, Benjamin, 111
Barr, Bob, on surveillance, 26
Berlin Wall, collapse of, 1
Berlusconi, Silvio, 93
bin Laden, Osama, al-Qaeda network of, 5–6; Arab media turning on, 52; disappointment with, 48–54; favoring of, 45–48; hatred for United States by, 111; reportedly killed, 101
Blair, Tony, international cooperation and, 12
Bloomberg, Michael, 119–21
Bohlen, Celestine, 95
box cutters, airplanes and, 18
Buddhism, Tibetan, Gere, Richard, and, 107
budget, Social Security funds for, 32; terrorism and, 20
Bush, George W., anti-terrorism policies of, 22, 26; Democrats and, 19; election of, 11; Enron and, 37–38; foreign policy agenda of, 3; pledge to New York by, 119; popularity of, 26–27; retaliation justification by, 83; war against terrorism and, 14–15
Bush, George, Sr., "New World Order" and, 2

capitalism, 6; European support for, 11; triumph of, 1
Carry, Jim, donation by, 110
Carter, Jimmy, 1
Carville, James, political impact of September 11 and, 19, 20
celebrities, donations by, 108; modesty and, 108–10

Chamber of Commerce, 118
Chechnya, United States criticism on, 9
Cheney, Dick, 35, 37
Chertoff, Michael, 36
China, al-Qaeda funding of terrorism in, 15; Tibetan oppression and trade with, 1; United Sates relationship with, 15
Chomsky, Noam, 74
Churchill, Winston, 62
Clinton, Bill, 24, 94
cockpit doors, 28
Cold War, ix; democracy promotion in, 1
Colombian drug kings, 15
Community of Democracies conference, 2
corporations, tax breaks for, 34
cultures, guilt, 85–90; popular, after September 11, xii, 103–16; shame, 85–90

Daschle, Tom, 20, 34, 37
democracy, Athens and, 68, 72; promotion of, 1–3, 7, 17; triumph of liberal, 1
Democrats, 19–21; Bush, George W., and, 19
Dinkins, David, 123
domestic policy, changes in, x
donations, celebrities and, 108; telethon and, 114–16
Dreamworks, 117
Dreyfus Affair, Péguy, Charles, on, 64

e-mail, monitoring of, 23
education, in Afghanistan, funding of, 17; in United States, 18
effeminacy, 91–92
egalitarianism, 71
Emmy awards, postponement of, 113
Enron Corporation, Bush, George W.,

contacts with, 37–38; collapse of, 35–38

European allies, complications with, 13; United States and, 10–11

Fascism, 41
federal employees, firing of, 29
Fleischer, Ari, 35
Foreign Intelligence Security Act, 23
Foreign policy, approval of, 7; Bush, George W., and, 3; changes in, x; practical and philosophical guide to, 3
free trade, international, European support in, 11
Fukuyama, Frances, 1
fundamentalism, Islamic, 98

G7 summits, abandoning of, 5
Gere, Richard, Tibetan Buddhism and, 107
Giuliani, Rudolph, accomplishments of, xii, 119–25; response to terrorist attack by, xii, 123–24; strengths and weaknesses of, 122
global capitalism, European support in, 11
Gore, Al, election of, 11
Green, Mark, 119–21
Greenberg, Stanley, political impact of September 11 and, 19, 20
ground crew area, airport, security in, 30
Ground Zero, tourist attraction and, 132
Guantanamo Bay, prisoners of, 6, 11, 13
guilt cultures, 85–90
Gulf War, end of, 2

Hanks, Tom, 110, 112
Harrell, David, 93
Hart, Gary, terrorism and, 2
Hawn, Goldie, 103–4, 111

Hitchens, Christopher, 109
Holdich, Colonel Sir Thomas Hungerford, 62
Hollings, Ernest, 38
Hollywood, changes in, 115–16; present-day populism in, 116; terrorism and, 103–16
human rights activists, United States foreign policy and, 1
human rights records, assessment of, 1
Huntington, Samuel, 2
Husayn, Adil, 43
Hussein, Saddam, 84

ideological struggle, end of, 1
India, sanctions placed on, 1; United States relationship with, 4
Indian parliament, Kashmiri terrorist attack on, 4
Indyk, Martin, 51
international free trade, European support in, 11
Internet, monitoring of, 23, 24; rural access to, 35
Iranian hostage crisis, 77, 98, 100
Iraq, invasion of Kuwait by, 2; war over oil with, 112
Islam, aftermath of September 11 on, xi; bin Laden, Osama, and, 45–48; fundamentalism in, 98; hatred of United States by, 42–45; history of, 40–42; hostility by, 42; Musharraf, Pervez and, 53; Yemen and, 53
Israel, economy of, 7; psyche of, 7; United States relationship with, 4
Italian mafia, 15

Jibril, Ahmad, American fatalities and, 43
Jospin, Lionel, 11
junk bond, military-industrial-corporate complex and, 111

Kahdir, Hussam, 46
Kashmiri, al-Qaeda funding of
terrorism in, 15; terrorist attack on
Indian parliament by, 4
Katzof, Rabbi Irwin, 105
Kennedy, John, military-industrial-
corporate complex and, 111
Kenya, U.S. Embassy bombing of, 78,
94
Khomeini, Ayatollah, 42, 55
knives, on airplanes, 28
Kramer, Martin, 41
Kuwait, Iraqi invasion of, 2

LaGuardia, Fiorello, 122
Lansing, Sherry, 113
Leahy, Patrick, 27
Lebanon, U.S. Marine barracks
bombing in, 77–78
Lewis, Bernard, 91
liberal democracy, triumph of, 1
Lowry, Rich, 82
Lugar, Richard, 33

Maher, Bill, 94, 110
marshals, on airplanes, 28
Marxism-Leninism, 41
McAuliffe, Terry, 37
McElvaine, Robert, 92
Milosevic, Slobodan, 84
missile defense system, creation of, 9
Muhammad, Faqir, 62
Muhammad, Sufi, 50
multiculturalism, 74
Musharraf, Pervez, speech attacking
militant Islam by, 53
Muslim(s), bin Laden, Osama, and,
46; career of, 40; children, 115;
sense of failure, 40–41

Nader, Ralph, election of, 11, 121
nail files, confiscation of, 102
NATO, creation of, 1; expansion of,

1, 9; peace-keeping operations in
Balkans by, 1
Nazism, 83
Netanyahu, Binyamin, 74
New York, Bush, George, W., pledge
to, 119; coping with September 11,
126–27; deficit and, 119; disaster in,
127; economic damage in, 118–19;
flyers of missing people in, 131–32;
heroes in, viii, 129–33; response to
terrorist attacks by, viii, 121–22
New York City Partnership, 118
newspapers, coverage of terrorist
attack by, 122–23
Nixon, Richard, military-industrial-
corporate complex and, 111;
Vietnam War and, 83
Noonan, Peggy, on terrorism, 2, 91
November 9, September 11 v., 54–55
Nuclear Non-Proliferative
bureaucracy, 5
nuclear war, terrorism and, 2
nuclear weapons, sanctions placed on
India and, 1; sanctions placed on
Pakistan and, 1

Office of Emergency Management,
creation of, 126
Omar, Mullah Muhammad, 76

Pakistan, sanctions placed on, 1;
United States relationship with, 4
Pan-Arabism, 41
Pan-Syrianism, 41
Paramount Pictures, 113
Pataki, George, 119
patriotism, Americans and, 98–101;
Hollywood and, 105–8; and USA
Patriot Act, 21–22, 22–27
Péguy, Charles, Dreyfus Affair and,
63–64
Peloponnesian War, 62; history of, 67
"pen-register," 23–24

Pericles, models of freedom from, 67–
74; plague in Athens and, 62; vision
of society by, 73
Pinter, Harold, 74
policy implications of United States,
55–59; consequences of, 55–56
post–Cold War, 2
POW's, Guantanamo Bay prisoners
as, 11–12
power, mortality of, 76
Putin, Valdimir, 9; Lord Robertson
meeting with, 9–10

Reagan, Ronald, 84
Reid, Richard, 102
relief work, money for, 33
Renaissance, laws of honor in, 87
Roberts, Julia, 113
Robertson, Lord, Putin, Valdimir,
meeting with, 9–10
Rockaway Beach, Queens, jetliner
crash into, 125
Rosett, Claudia, 7
Russia, American war on terrorism
supported by, 9; United States
relationship with, 10

Sabri, Ikrama, 42–43
Said, Edward, 74
Saletan, William, 7
satellite television, 10, 20
Saudi Arabia, U.S. military barracks
bombing in, 78; war over oil with,
112
screening stations, airport, 102
security, Aviation and Transportation
Security Act and, 21; baggage areas,
30; confiscation of nail files by, 102;
Foreign Intelligence Security Act
and, 23; ground crew areas and, 30;
United States and, 16–17, 23–24
September 11, aftermath of, ix, 77;
Carville, James, on, 20; events of,

119–21; goals of, 56–57; New York
coping with, 126–27; November 9
v., 54–55; popular culture after,
103–16; Shrum, Robert, on, 19;
telethon for, 112–14
shame cultures, 85–90
Shariat-e-Mohammedi, Tehrik Nifaz,
50
Sharon, Ariel, 13
Sheidlower, Jesse, 95
Shrum, Robert, political impact of
September 11 and, 19, 20
Social Security funds, budget surplus
and, 32
Sontag, Susan, 74
Sorkin, Aaron, 110, 111
South Asia, United States
negotiations in, 15
Soviet Union, collapse of, 9; satellite
launch by, 18
stegonagraphy, 26
stimulus bill, 21, 22, 31–35
Stone, Oliver, 109, 111
Streisand, Barbara, 106–7, 111
struggle, ideological, end of, 1
surveillance, 26

Taliban, 17; collapse of, 5, 48
Tanzania, U.S. Embassy bombing of,
78, 94
tax breaks, corporations and, 34
telethon, September 11, 112–14
terrorism, al-Qaeda funding of, 15;
American reaction to, 110; budget
and, 20; Bush, George, W., war
against, 14–15; cowardness of, 96–
99; Hart, Gary on, 2; Hollywood
and, 109; Indian parliament and, 4;
international investigation in
financing of, 3, 11; investigations,
sharing information of, 23; missile-
guided sort of, 3; new ways in
fighting of, 16; New York response

terrorism (*continued*)
to, viii, 121–22; newspaper
coverage of, 122–23; Noonan,
Peggy on, 2, 91; nuclear war and, 2;
Russia's support for America
against, 9; surprise of, ix, 9; United
States response to, ix; USS *Cole*
and, 78, 94; West Jerusalem and, 7
Thucydides, 67
Tibet, oppression of, trade with
China and, 1
Tibetan Buddhism, Gere, Richard,
and, 107
"trap and trace," 23–24
Turabi, Hasan at-, 45
Twin Towers. *See* World Trade
Center

Unilateralism, 16; intelligent, 16–17
United Nations (U.N.), 1
United States of America Patriot Act,
21–22, 22–27
United States, al-Qaeda operations in,
22–23, 56–57; Chechnya criticized
by, 9; education in, 18; European
allies and, 10–11; foreign policy of,
1; India's relationship with, 4;
Islamic hatred toward, 42–45;
Israel's relationship with, 4; Jibril,
Ahmad, and, 43; military power in,
48–50, 75; new threats against, 2;
Pakistan relationship with, 4; policy
implications by, 55–59; Russia's
relationship with, 10; Russia's
support against terrorism in, 9;
security in, 16–17, 23–24; response

to terrorism by, ix, 110;
unilateralism in, 16; wealth in, 75;
Western Europe's relationship
with, 4. *See also* Americans
U.S.-backed Northern Alliance, 48
U.S. Embassy, Kenya's bombing of,
78, 94; Tanzania's bombing of, 78,
94
U.S. Marine barracks, Lebanon
bombing of, 78
U.S. military barracks, Saudi Arabia
bombing of, 78
USA Patriot Act, 21–22, 22–27
USS *Cole*, terrorist attack on, 78, 94

Vietnam War, military-industrial-
corporate complex and, 111; Nixon,
Richard, and, 83

Warsaw, Community of Democracies
conference in, 2
Waters, Maxine, racial/ethnic
minorities and, 26
West Bank, occupation of, 13–14
West Jerusalem, terrorism on, 7
Western Europe, United States
relationship with, 4
wiretaps, 23
Wodehouse, P.G., 65
women, democracy in Athens and, 68
Woolsey, James, 25
World Trade Center, bombing of
(1993), 24, 78, 126; combing
through rubble of, 132–33

Yemen, Islamic foreigners in, 53;